2-Minute Pep Talks

67 Jolts of Inspiration for More Hope, Comfort, and Love in Any Situation

Niklas Göke

365 Publishing

2-Minute Pep Talks: 67 Jolts of Inspiration for More Hope, Comfort, and Love in Any Situation

Copyright © 2022 by Niklas Göke

All rights reserved. No part of this book may be reproduced in any form without written permission from the author. Any brief, quoted passages must be in line with appropriate sourcing standards.

ISBN Ebook: 978-3-949824-03-6

ISBN Paperback: 978-3-949824-04-3

ISBN Hardcover: 978-3-949824-05-0

To Iris, Knut, and Riccarda

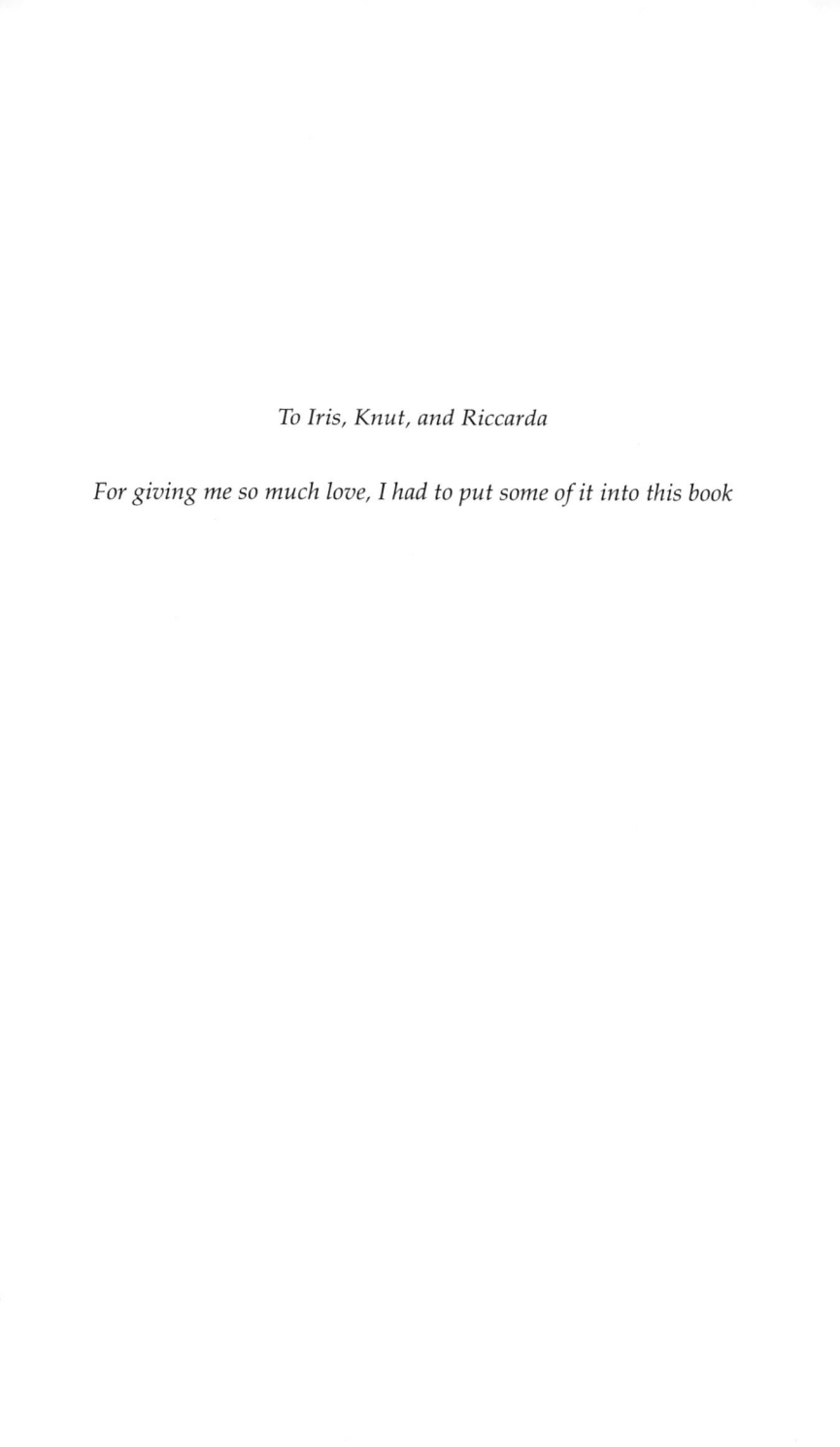

For giving me so much love, I had to put some of it into this book

Table of Contents

Introduction	ix
A Word About Pep Talks	xiii

Part I
Comfort

Mirror Speech	3
You're Still Here	4
Out of Character	6
Mister Rogers	8
You Can't Uncut This Corner	11
The $100 Bill	13
Time Billionaire	15
Life's Biggest Paradox	17
Last-Second Thoughts	19
Your Thoughts Are Yours	21
Your Brain Is Your Ally, Not Your Enemy	23
Seeing Is Solving	25
Muddy Water	27
Don't Forget to Inhale	29

Part II
Work

The Easiest Job in the World	33
For the Jacks	36
What Do You Hate Not Doing?	39
The 3 Fs of Mastery	41
Option 1 of 1	43
Don't 80/20 Your Dream	45
Working on What Matters	48
The Most Valuable Skill in the World	49
Public Speaking for the Rest of Us	52
Seneca's LinkedIn	54
Human Communication 101	56
Perseverance	59

Part III
(Tough) Love

If You Want the Zig, Accept the Zag	65
Accept or Convince	67
Happiness Is Third Grade Math	69
You Don't Need a New Thing to Be Grateful For	72
Pericles	74
The Secret	76
2 Kinds of Comfort	78
Don't Wait	80
How You Do Anything Is How You Do Everything	82
On Taking the Stairs	84
Why Birds Fly	86
Gossip Girl 1813	88
Reunion	91
You Don't Need New Friends	94
The 30% Rule	96
The 4 Monks	99

Part IV
Reminders

Don't Forget Your Light Today	103
Life's Worst Trap	106
Relationships = Trains	108
Through Wrong to Right	111
The Isms That Ruin Your Judgement	112
Don't Listen to the Ducks	115
4 More Isms	118
You Can't Outrun Yourself	121
The Secret of a Happy Life	123
Are You Free to Abstain?	126
Your Phone Should Be Like Your Toothbrush	128
When the Phone Rings	131
Shibuya	134
Be Water, My Friend	136

Part V
Hope

How To Not Waste Your Life	141
If You Can't Beat the Fear, Just Do It Scared	144
Someone Will Save You Today	146
One More Time	148

If You're Not Valued, You're in the Wrong Place	151
Change Is Resistance	153
The Meaning of Life	154
Your Best Thought	157
Now Would Be a Great Time to Give Up	160
Tomorrow Can Be a Good Day	163
Pep Talk	165
What's Next?	169
About the Author	171
Footnotes	173

Introduction

Pep talks are like vitamins: You can take them every day preemptively, or you can wait until your body signals a lack of them — but sooner or later, you *will* need your vitamins.

Vitamins aren't steroids. Their purpose is not to boost you beyond what you are capable of. They merely restore your body's natural balance. When it comes to pep talks, the balance they maintain is not your health but your spirit.

When we are young, our spirits run high all the time. As we grow up, we lose some, sometimes *all*, of the youthful glow of optimism, but not for a lack of trying. Drugs, entertainment, we might use all kinds of addictions and distractions in hopes of regaining our zest for life, but in the end, they always come up short — because as with steroid injections, the effects from a temporary solution can't last forever.

According to thinker Prachi Nain, we don't need to inject anything into our lives in the first place. We simply need to get back to our natural, high-spirited state. "A good pep talk doesn't load you up with something that doesn't belong to you," Nain writes.[1] It simply removes "the built-up layers of self-doubt and fear."

Don't think of a pep talk like an energy gel handed to a marathoner mid-run to eke out an extra mile, Nain suggests. Think of it "like taking away a heavy backpack." Like removing a weight from your shoulders. That's what this book is for.

2-Minute Pep Talks is here to take off your backpack or, at the very least, remind you to take it off yourself. Drop the emotional baggage that doesn't serve you, and you'll thrive thanks to the feeling of lightness that remains. What is that feeling made of? Hope, love, and comfort, mostly. Often in reverse order.

When you start your day from comfort, it won't anxiously shake you awake at 7:05 in the morning, yelling, "You're late! You're already late!" into your ear. Comfort will wake you up slowly and protect your sense of calm. As a result, you'll feel safe and level-headed — just what you need to make good decisions.

Love, on the other hand, will forever transform your work and relationships, but only if it's an ever-present force. Love will make you confident yet humble. You will ask life for no less than you deserve, but you'll also never forget to empathize, share with, and help others along the way — because being there for others *is* the way, not just to the things we want but also to the very love we seek.

And hope? Nothing in life ever gets accomplished without hope. Hope is the driving force of humanity. Without hope, none of us would get up in the morning, no matter how relentlessly fear and other negative emotions might ring in our ears. As long as we *do* hope, however, not even despair itself can keep us from getting dressed, opening our door, and taking a step. It might only be *one* step, one tiny step of progress, but to keep the future alive, one step is always enough.

The challenge with your spirit is that it's not tied to your body. Unlike a sore throat or broken arm, you won't feel the cracks in your soul immediately. Our motivation can slip away slowly, but we rarely realize it. One day, we simply wake up and notice that it's gone. No hope. No love. No comfort. By that time, it takes a lot of work to restore our vitality, and a few months later, we'll likely repeat the same cycle.

In that sense, a daily pep talk is the ounce of prevention that, as Benjamin Franklin saw it, "is worth a pound of cure." You already know you need a pep talk *every now and then* — but if you get one every day, you'll never have to guess. That is the purpose of this book.

2-Minute Pep Talks is a collection of 67 jolts of inspiration for more comfort, love, and hope in any situation. Why 67? Because according to science, on average, it takes 66 days to form a habit.[2] Add one for good luck, and you've got the daily vitamin practice you need in order to not lose your balance.

By the time you're done with this book, you can start it over or turn to other sources of inspiration. Either way, you'll have built a new pattern: You will start every day with a call upon your relentlessly positive, forever forward-looking, uniquely human spirit.

A Word About Pep Talks
(And This Book)

Let's briefly establish what makes a good pep talk.

According to science, it must contain three elements, which we can easily remember with the all-too-apt acronym "PEP:" purpose, empathy, and prescription.[1]

Purpose connects the challenge in front of you to the big picture. Why is it important to you to write a novel, be a good parent, or sell more Tupperware than any other sales rep? The more clearly you can see the reward — and usually the more it involves helping other people — the easier it will be to persevere. A good pep talker will remind you of your purpose or, at the very least, get you to remember the one only you know about.

Empathy is about recognizing your struggle. "I know what you're going through, and you are not alone. Others have walked this path before you. Even you have. Remember that one time you stood up for yourself? Beat the odds? Kept going anyway? You can do it again. I believe in you." Almost all pep talks hit the "I believe in you" mark, but that least requires empathy. We want our leaders to understand us more so than rally us, and only if they demonstrate said understanding will their words sound truly inspiring.

Prescription, or direction, as the researchers call it, is about using "uncertainty-reducing language." When we are afraid primarily because we don't know what to do, clear instructions can work wonders. Which tool, rule, or framework you need, however, is highly situation-dependent. Therefore, the pep talk giver must know exactly what you're dealing with.

Some of the pep talks in this book will lean more on prescription, others more on purpose. We might not always talk about your exact cause or situation, but we'll consider lots of specific examples and muse a good bit about the meaning of life — and what bigger purpose could there possibly be? My biggest goal, however, is for empathy to be ever-present throughout this book, not just for me to show compassion to you, but also for you to be more compassionate with yourself.

So much for the science. Here's what *I* believe a good pep talk must do.

First, a good pep talk is always positive. It mustn't sugarcoat the truth, but it should always end on a high note. In fact, the very *best* pep talks *use* the truth to show us a new perspective which, in turn, refills our batteries. Empowered with a different approach we can't wait to try, we storm back out on the field. Meanwhile, the football team whose coach threatens it with a beating should they lose the game is not really a team that wants to win. It is a team that is scared to lose. Some people may try to motivate through fear, but that is not what we will be doing here.

Second, like the word "pep," the talk needs to be short. If you steep green tea for more than two minutes, some of its health benefits will disappear. It will also taste bitter, like a look at the clock after you've watched 17 motivational videos in a row. Inspiration is a perishable good. That's why most of the pep talks in this book are two-minute reads: short and sometimes sweet, but always full of perspective. Ideally, you'll read one, put the book down, and tackle whatever you need to tackle — or, if you're *actually* playing football, *whoever* you need to tackle.

Finally, a pep talk must always match the problem and mood of the day. We don't always know exactly what we need, and that's why it helps to have a wide selection of pep talks available. Therefore, in the pages of this book, you'll find pep talks to help you overcome fear, pep talks to give you hope, and pep talks to give you comfort. There are pep talks about work, about happiness, and about friendship. There are even pep talks about your phone, about public speaking, and about taking the stairs. In short, there's a pep talk for almost any situation. I hope you'll find the one you need, and I've grouped them into five not-necessarily-in-order sections to that end:

1. **Comfort** is about being at peace with the world and yourself, exactly as you are today.
2. **Work** will deliver motivation, but it will also light the path towards discovering, creating, doing the job you'll never find on LinkedIn: the work you were born to do.
3. **(Tough) Love** will provide new perspectives on things you've always known, while…
4. **Reminders** will simply bring back some truths you need but might have forgotten.
5. **Hope** wants to be nothing less than your springboard to the stars, even when the night feels dark and shrouded in mystery.

A Word About Pep Talks

While you can read this book one chapter per day and thus try to build a daily pep talk habit, there really are no rules about order and timeline here. Welcome to the pep talk–multiverse. Maybe you'll begin at the beginning. Maybe you'll begin at the end. You can jump to whatever chapter sounds most interesting or flip to a random page. You can also read this book one page at a time, one chapter per week, or cover to cover in one go. At 67 pep talks of two minutes each, that last option still amounts to less procrastination than watching an *Avengers* movie — I checked. The only rule of this book is that you should feel inspired by the time you put it down.

You're too important to not believe you can take on the world. I want you to begin every day fully convinced that you can — because *you can*.

Here goes my first attempt.

Part I
Comfort

"Reading was my escape and my comfort, my consolation, my stimulant of choice: reading for the pure pleasure of it, for the beautiful stillness that surrounds you when you hear an author's words reverberating in your head."

— *Paul Auster*

Mirror Speech

For his Walk of Fame star, Snoop Dogg thanked all the usual suspects. Then, he went off script for 30 seconds:

"I want to thank me. I want to thank me for believing in me. I want to thank me for doing all this hard work. I want to thank me for having no days off. I want to thank me for never quitting. I want to thank me for always being a giver and trying to give more than I receive. I want to thank me for trying to do more right than wrong. I want to thank me for just being me at all times."

Invest those same 30 seconds in front of your mirror today. Thank yourself. Yesterday is gone. Today is alive. You're still here, and that's all that matters.

You're Still Here

You were born as an accident. Or during an accident. Or *with* an accident. You were definitely born through great pain and suffering. But you're still here.

You were raised in a poor home. A dysfunctional home. A home that clipped your wings and left you with deep scars you had to mend much later. But you're still here.

You had a tough childhood. You were the runt of the litter. The middle child. The big brother with all the pressure. Maybe, you were all alone. But you're still here.

You didn't always get what you wanted. The other kids in school were mean. The boys never called back. The teachers had it in for you. But you're still here.

You wasted a lot of time growing up. You couldn't figure out what you really wanted. You dealt with disease, disadvantage, depression. But you're still here.

You were rejected when you put yourself out there. You showed vulnerability and honesty and compassion, and someone else spat in your face. But you're still here.

Your company failed. So did the big event at work, the 5th

grade dance recital, and the opening of your art gallery. But you're still here.

You made a mistake. You know you messed up, and you know it's your fault. You don't even know how to fix it. You just know you feel like you have to. But you're still here.

Your body never gives you an easy time. It won't lose weight when it should. It doesn't want you to be fit and lean and healthy. It craves junk food and ice cream and popcorn. But you're still here.

You've inherited your dad's gambling problem. Or your mom's excessive spending habits. You struggle to make rent, to save money, to keep your dollar bills together. But you're still here.

You don't know how to be happy. Life is confusing. It's big and complicated and there are way too many options for everything. But you're still here.

Life is and sometimes it isn't. But it's short for all of us. It's a unique and crazy experience, and there are no do-overs, no second season, no late-night rerun tickets.

Every day is special. A once-in-a-lifetime chance. Another reason to be grateful. And you're still here. So today is a good day.

Out of Character

Mike Ross has a photographic memory, and yet, he keeps losing his phone. The first time I watched *Suits*, I didn't understand why. It seemed odd. A misplaced trait in a genius character. How could the writers have missed this? How did this anomaly slip through the cracks?

The more I watched, the more I understood: The writers didn't *miss* this flaw. They put it there. Mike's flaws are what keep him interesting. Mike Ross is a good man whom bad things have happened to. He's a lawyer but not a real one. He's loyal but naïve. Mike is full of conflict.

In other words, Mike Ross is *human*. Mike is madly, deeply, purely in love with Rachel, and yet, he starts an affair with another woman. Mike can outwit any intellectual attacker, but he still lets himself get blackmailed. That's unlike him, but that's what we do, isn't it?

We fall out of character — and that's what keeps us interesting.

We all have this idea of who we want to be. The perfect version of our character. Of course, we'll never get there. We take the odd highway exit here and there. We do things we can't make sense of in hindsight, and then, much later still, we suddenly can.

There's this quote that "what you do when you don't have to will determine who you'll be when you can't help it." Why did we leave our perfectly comfortable life for a much harder one? Why did we disappoint the person we love? How did we get here? Did we choose so? Did life choose us?

It's tempting to want to eliminate chance. To iron out the flaws in our character. There's no way to succeed, but even if there was, it'd only set us up for failure on a much grander scale. Who wants to be 100% predictable? Life's too fast to stop changing. No rule can last forever. Falling out of character keeps us — keeps *life* — interesting.

That doesn't mean we shouldn't fight hard to be our best selves. In fact, we'll always *have to*. But we'll also pull an odd move every now and then. That's something to celebrate, not regret. At the very least, we should accept it.

When you forget your phone, call the wrong person, or miss the deadline you never miss, don't beat yourself up for being unpredictable. Don't cast stones into the mirror.

Remember you are human. Trust that the detour will eventually make sense. Forgive yourself, then get back into the picture. You're a star, after all — and the show must go on.

Mister Rogers

Mister Rogers' Neighborhood was one of the longest-running children's TV shows of all time. For over 30 years, Fred Rogers used stories and songs to guide preschoolers through everyday interactions with other people, showing them what it means to be human, and how to do it gracefully. In hindsight, it's hard to believe the program almost didn't happen.

In 1969, president Lyndon Johnson proposed a $20 million bill for the creation of PBS, the Public Broadcasting Service. Before the bill could pass in the Senate, however, Richard Nixon took office — and promptly suggested to cut the funding in half. Mister Rogers was chosen to testify in a hearing regarding this matter.

Rogers made some good points, for example that $6,000, the current budget of one 30-minute episode of his show, might otherwise only pay for less than two minutes of cartoons.[1] His best argument by far, however, had little to do with facts and figures. It was a point about feelings, a point Rogers made with the lyrics of one of his songs:

What do you do with the mad that you feel
When you feel so mad you could bite?
When the whole wide world seems oh so wrong
And nothing you do seems very right?

What do you do? Do you punch a bag?
Do you pound some clay or some dough?
Do you round up friends for a game of tag?
Or see how fast you go?

It's great to be able to stop
When you've planned a thing that's wrong,
And be able to do something else instead
And think this song:

I can stop when I want to
Can stop when I wish
I can stop, stop, stop any time.
And what a good feeling to feel like this
And know that the feeling is really mine.
Know that there's something deep inside
That helps us become what we can.
For a girl can be someday a lady
And a boy can be someday a man.

Not only did Mister Rogers' presentation move the usually hard-boiled and grumpy chairman of the hearing, Senator John Pastore, to tears, it also secured the entire $20 million in funding, guaranteeing the future of his and other educational kid's TV shows for decades to come.

That's what Rogers wanted to do: give children a good education right in the comfort of their home. Thankfully, his understanding of education went beyond math and history. It also included *feelings*.

"Anything that is mentionable can be more manageable," Rogers once said. The twist is that "anything that's human is mentionable." There is nothing we *can't* openly discuss, and when we do, even the heaviest burden gets lighter. "When we can talk about our feelings, they become less overwhelming, less upsetting, and less scary."

"If we in public television can only make it clear that feelings are mentionable and manageable, we will have done a great service for mental health," Rogers said as part of his plea. Mentionable and manageable. That's what feelings are, he believed.

That was more than 50 years ago, in a time when the term "mental health" was basically unheard of, *especially* with regards to children. Today, it is a topic widely discussed, thanks in part to his remarks.

The message, however, will forever remain one we must both hear and spread: No matter what you feel, it is okay to have this feeling. You can mention it. You can manage it. And you don't have to do either alone. Welcome to the neighborhood.

You Can't Uncut This Corner

Maybe you were in a hurry. Maybe you were desperate for a win. Maybe everything already went wrong that day, so you decided to take one for yourself.

Whatever it was, you knew you were taking a shortcut when you did it. You knew that wasn't the end of the line. That the right ticket would've been more expensive. The answer you gave wasn't supposed to help, it was supposed to *get you off the hook*.

I get it. The world's too big. It's easy. There are too many opportunities. Too many corners one can cut. Sooner or later, we all do. I have. You have. Most of us will cut many corners over the course of our lives.

It feels good at first, doesn't it? "Ha, I got away with it!" Eventually, however, that smug feeling will turn into a smudge, a stain on your shirt you can't get off. It's true: What's done is done. That stain will stay forever.

No matter how small they are, each of our shameful shortcuts will always remain a scar upon our backs. But if we don't add any new ones, with time, they'll begin to fade.

If you wash your shirt often enough, only a remnant will be left. A little reminder of a stain that once was. You'll still see its outline, but you won't remember how it got there, and that's when you'll know: You've finally forgotten how to cut that kind of corner.

There is, by definition, no fast track to not cutting corners. Being careful is what it's all about. You have to be mindful of each corner when you get there. That takes slowness, deliberation, and patience. These are attitudes we must practice, not just once but every day.

Yes, the world is big. So many corners you could cut. But it's also big enough to *go around them*. There's always room to take the right path or forge one if you have to. Slow down. Take it easy. Don't hurt yourself.

You can't uncut this corner. But you can not cut the next one.

The $100 Bill

One day, the teacher brought a $100 bill to school. She showed it to the class and asked: "How much is this worth?"

"$100," the class said in unison.

The teacher crumpled up the bill, then held it in the palm of her hand. Once again, she asked: "How much is this worth?"

"$100," the students said.

The teacher threw the bill on the ground and asked: "How much is it worth now?"

At first, the students gasped, but then they shrugged and said: "Well, it's still $100."

Furiously, the teacher stomped on the bill several times. Then, she asked: "And now? What's the value of it now?"

The students looked at each other incredulously and said: "Come on! It's still $100!"

Finally, the teacher broke into a smile. "Good!" she said. "Remember this lesson. Not just with money, but in life as well."

"Whatever happens, however people treat you, you are as valuable today as you were yesterday, and you will be as valuable tomorrow and every day henceforth."

"Remember to love yourself as you are. Your circumstances may change, but your value will not."

———

Life offers endless chances to doubt yourself. It's easy to crumble when people stomp on you. It takes courage to get up, straighten yourself, and say: "I'm still a $100 bill. My worth is still the same."

Some people will try to chip away little pieces, and sometimes, life will nearly tear you apart. But as long as you get up again, you'll always be left standing — and there's no wrinkle a little ironing can't fix.

You don't need to look your best each day. You don't need to project your value at every turn. Just make sure you stay aware of it. You know your worth. That's all that matters. As long as *you* remember, everyone who truly needs to know already does.

As a human being, you have inherent, irrevocable, imperishable value. Know your worth, love yourself, and remember: Everyone loves a $100 bill — no matter how banged up it looks.

Time Billionaire

Would you rather have a billion dollars or a billion seconds?

If something takes you a million seconds to do, that's about 12 days. If you need a *billion* seconds, however, that's 31 *years* — not counting sleep.

Equating seconds to dollars, a billion dollars is worth 31 years of your time. Would you make that trade?

A reader once asked investor Anthony "Pomp" Pompliano a similar question: "If you could switch places with Warren Buffett, would you do it? You'd be one of earth's richest people, but you'd be 90 years old." In the money, yet out of time.

If you're in your 20s, you're a time multi-billionaire. You likely have more than two billion seconds left. If you're 50, you could *still* be a time billionaire. How much would Warren Buffett give to get back those seconds? Probably a lot more than a billion dollars.

"The time billionaires are the wealthiest among us, yet they fail to recognize the wealth they enjoy," Pomp writes.[1] "Having a billion dollars is great, but having a billion seconds is priceless. There is no amount of money in the world that can purchase immortality. Every human eventually runs out of time."

If you're young, Pomp says, perhaps you should think of yourself as wealthier than your older, financially richer peers:

"The time billionaire can have a time horizon that is counted in decades. The time billionaire can afford to be patient. The time billionaire can slowly compound money over time. There is no rush. There is no compressed timeline that clouds the judgement of a time billionaire. They can recover from almost any mistake. In a sense, the time billionaire is unshakeable."

If you're a time billionaire, don't fret about your lack of dollars. Embrace your advantage in time. Unlike the pieces of paper we all covet, we only get to spend our seconds once.

Life's Biggest Paradox

Towards the end of Marvel's *Dr. Strange*, our newly anointed hero must let go of his mentor. The Ancient One, a being who has protected time for thousands of years, is about to pass on, but not before giving Strange a final piece of advice.

Standing next to each other at a window looking out on a gigantic thunderstorm, Strange admits he is not ready for the big challenge he must face. "No one ever is," The Ancient One responds. "We don't get to choose our time."

And then, just before she fades away, she reveals something profound:

"Death is what gives life meaning. To know your days are numbered; your time is short."

The only reason our lives have meaning is that they *end*. The moment we are born, we're thrown onto an unstoppable curve of momentum, slingshotting towards the only definitive event in life — death.

Think about it: Everything that makes life great is fleeting.

Your ice cream tastes better because it's about to melt. Weekends with your partner are precious because you can only kiss them a finite number of times. Your grand mission to change the world is urgent because you don't know how long you have to accomplish it.

Every single experience that makes our time here worthwhile goes back to that time being over soon. No one wants to live forever once they've lived long enough, and yet dying is what we're most afraid of. It's the biggest paradox in life: Without death, it wouldn't mean anything.

The next time you drop your ice cream, suffer a broken heart, or have to let go of a dream, remember: Death is what gives life meaning. We may not get to choose our time, but every second passed is a second that made said time more precious — regardless of how you spent it.

Last Second Thoughts

Every year, some 15,000 people are injured in bus accidents in the United States.[1] Around 250 of them aren't lucky enough to walk away with a few scratches.

Imagine you cross the street, hear a noise, and look to the side. With only a split second left, you realize what's about to happen: A bus is going to hit you. You have time for just one last thought. What will it be?

Given the short notice, you might default to one of two universal options: "Okay" or, well, "Sh*t."

While your ultimate reaction will be more about the bus and less about your past, I do think it would be somewhat gut-informed — a faint but relevant indicator of how you've lived your life thus far.

One last-second thought is the equivalent of "Thank you," a sign that you've done the best you could have done, given what you had. "Okay, a bus is going to hit me. It is what it is, and let's see what happens." That sounds to me like someone who's at peace. Someone who's grateful for the incredible experience of life as a human being, regardless of how long it may have been and whether it might end right now. Someone who, like all of us, would probably change a bunch of things if they could do it over, but not so much as to willingly swap places with just about anyone sitting on the bus.

The other last impression is the kind uttered by anyone who realizes it's too late for something important: "Damn! I haven't done this thing, and now, I'm gonna get steamrolled. I'm not ready! Give me more time!" It is a symptom of chances left untaken, words left unspoken, and potential left unfulfilled. You could have done so much more in the time you had — but you didn't. And it is only now, in this last second, that, much like the bus, it hits you.

Think about anyone you believe is living a great life. Chances are, it's a life full of failure. The road behind them is littered with wrecks. Crashed cars. Broken dreams. Failed projects. Maybe even a bus or two. And yet, they've still arrived where they are. Despite all their problems, challenges, and mistakes, they still manage to live a life you admire.

Now think about someone whose life you believe is filled with regret. Do you envy them? Do you think they're living their best life? Can you think of another regretful person? How about a third? Is there anyone like that who you would trade places with? Anyone at all?

Even if *you're* its cause, at the end of the day, failure is always an external event that happens to you. Regret, however, is an activity. It's a terrible pastime we *decide* to engage in. Failure is a consequence of living we cannot avoid. Regret is a state we can only choose. One is inevitable, the other just a waste of time.

You'll never do it all perfectly, but try to do it gracefully. Choose failure over regret, always. And please don't get hit by a bus.

Your Thoughts Are Yours

The prisoner can't leave his cell, but his thoughts are his.
The student must sit in class, but her thoughts are hers.
The teacher must give his lecture, but his thoughts are his.
The mother must feed her children, but her thoughts are hers.
The writer must stare at the screen, but his thoughts are his.
The therapist must listen, but her thoughts are hers.
The sprinter must lose the race, but his thoughts are his.
The patient must endure treatment, but her thoughts are hers.
The soldier can't see his family, but his thoughts are his.
The singer must take the stage, but her thoughts are hers.
The hero must make the sacrifice, but his thoughts are his.
The wanderer may get lost, but her thoughts are hers.

You will not get everything you want today. You may face pain, anger, frustration, or sadness. But through all this, your thoughts will be yours. No one can dictate the next sentence in your mind. That is for you alone to choose.

No matter what happens, no matter how good or bad it gets, this unique, human privilege is yours for the rest of your life. You can exercise it on top of the highest mountain or inside the darkest hole.

Over the course of your life, you will have *millions* of thoughts. Millions of chances to choose one that will serve you over another one that won't. It only takes *one* of those thoughts to acknowledge this gift. I can't make you think it. I can only remind you that you *can* — because your thoughts are yours.

What do you think?

Your Brain Is Your Ally, Not Your Enemy

It's a myth that we only use 10% of our brain,[1] but I can see why it's popular: It's the perfect excuse. "How can I excel if the tools I need to do so are in a place I can't access? If only there was a miracle drug..." In reality, even a single task can easily demand 35% of your brain's capacity,[2] and over the course of a single day, most of us will access all 100% — just different areas at different times.[3]

Still, many a movie has been made about said miracle drug, including *Limitless*, a film starring Bradley Cooper as a hard-up writer. After he discovers NZT-48, he finishes his book in a day, makes millions trading stocks, and enjoys his newfound life. Until the side effects kick in, that is. The movie is nice fuel for our daydreams, but it's also a wake-up call because, as Lars van der Peet says,[4] it reminds us "that we are unfulfilled potential, that we aren't doing everything we could and should be doing."

Our frustration with our brains shows on many levels: You might be angry that you can't remember what you wanted to say, feel sad that you can't solve an important problem, or watch *Limitless* because you can't find the energy to write your novel. As understandable as these frustrations are, they are born out of a misconception. Our brain was never something we were meant to have 100% control over. It is simply a partner we must work with.

There is no exact science on how much of our brain activity happens "below the surface," but it's a lot more than what we register and process in a conscious manner. Otherwise, we could neither function in a world so overflowing with sensory inputs nor perform any of our more complex behaviors, like driving a car or holding a conversation — let alone do both at the same time.

Whatever the exact ratio of subconscious-to-conscious activity, your brain is an iceberg: Most of it is under water. Your job is not to try and turn it upside down but to navigate whatever lies above sea level. Even the small terrain up top is constantly changing, and in order to maneuver it well, you must trust the iceberg to reveal the right part at the right time.

"Make your unconscious your ally instead of your enemy," Lars says. Accept that your brain requires breaks, and that in those breaks, your subconscious is working *for* you, not against you. Your mind can process even when you don't, and usually, it does its best work while you do none at all.

Your brain is not you. It will never define who you are, and yet, you must live with it every day. Treat your brain like a partner. You don't control them, but together, you can achieve a whole lot.

Towards the end of *Limitless*, the main character realizes he never needed a smart-drug in the first place. His limitations were mostly self-imposed. Instead of blaming his brain, he starts using it. That's the real message of the movie: We have everything we need. We just have to work with it rather than against it.

Seeing Is Solving

Once you become aware of a problem, your mind will try and solve it. It doesn't matter whether you want it to or not. Your subconscious does what it wants, and, luckily, it wants to find creative solutions to all kinds of challenges — so much so, in fact, that it can barely help itself.

That's why communication is key among teams, among friends, and among lovers. Humans can't consider what they don't know about, but everything they *do* know about will somehow be factored into the equation, if only at a subconscious level.

If you flag your overwhelm at work, you likely won't be fired without warning. Bring up an issue with group dynamic, and you'll also bring all your friends to the table. Why? Our brains can't resist a good problem. No matter who shares which issue, they want to latch on to it. They want to be part of the solution.

That's why humans are, at heart, cooperative creatures. We love rallying together, if not for the sense of community, then at least to quench our individual brains' thirst for overcoming a meaningful challenge.

We have a saying in Germany: "Sorrow shared is sorrow halved." Similarly, a problem shared is a problem half-solved.

Like mould in a jar, problems can only grow in the darkest, dampest corners of our minds. As soon as we open up, the sunlight will dry and shrink them. From there, it is only a matter of time until they fall apart.

Whatever your struggles, drag them into other people's periphery. Seeing is solving. Problems only persist while they're invisible. Don't keep the lid on for too long.

Muddy Water

Once upon a time, the Buddha was traveling from one town to the next with his disciples. They happened to pass a small lake, and when they did, the Buddha turned to one of his followers: "I am thirsty. Please get me some water from the lake."

The disciple walked down to the water, but when he reached it, he noticed an ox cart had just begun crossing the lake. In the cart's wake, the water turned brown and murky. The student returned to the Buddha and said: "The water is muddy. I'm afraid it is unfit to drink. Should we keep moving to find another lake?"

Surprisingly, the thirsty Buddha said: "No. Let us take a rest here."

An hour later, the Buddha once again asked the disciple to get water. He went back to the lake and found the water was clear. The mud had settled down and the water on top looked clean and drinkable. He collected some in a pot and brought it to the Buddha.

When the student gave him the water, the Buddha said, "See? You let the water be, and the mud settled down on its own. You got clear water, and it didn't require any effort. Your mind is the same. Do nothing, and its disturbances will disappear."

Your mind is a tool better than magic. It has the power to perceive everything in this vast, dynamic, fast-paced world we live in. It can decode any problem or situation, break it down into its parts, and piece it back together.

Your mind can even imagine what it's like to do all this from someone else's perspective, *even if* that person is someone who never existed at all. It can dream up places, ideas, and characters, and travel to distant planets without you so much as leaving your chair — but when the water is muddy, your mind can't do any of those things.

Sometimes, the powerful force in our head goes haywire. It zones in on the wrong problem, the wrong person, or the wrong idea and clamps up. Like a dog with a bone, it will desperately cling to a thought that doesn't serve you, or run in all directions at the same time without you moving an inch.

This happens to all of us. Don't fight it. You'll only make it worse. Instead, remember the Buddha: "Let's take a rest here." Sleep. Relax. Have a cup of tea. Give it some time. The mud will settle down.

Being calm isn't the result of trying not to be frantic. It is the result of not trying at all.

Don't stir the muddy water. Don't mess with an already messy mind. Let it be, and soon, the water will once again be clear.

Don't Forget to Inhale

Living is exhaling.

You wake up, open your eyes, and jump out of bed. You brush teeth, get dressed, and race to the breakfast table. Phew!

You work. You type. You work harder. You type faster. Pheeew.

You buy groceries. You sort your bills. You tuck your kid in. Pheeeeeeeew.

You watch Netflix. You doomscroll. You listen to a friend yap for hours. Phew, phew, pheeeeeeeeeeeew.

By the time your head hits the pillow, you are exhausted. You're wheezing. What happened? Simple: You forgot to inhale. That's *also* living.

Matthew Inman says creativity is like breathing: "When you make stuff, you're exhaling. But you can't exhale forever. Eventually, you have to breathe in. Or you'll be dead."

It's not just creativity. It's everything. The adulting. The job you're trying to be good at. Even the experiencing of awesome things. As long as you're doing, you're exhaling. But eventually, you have to breathe in. Or you'll be dead.

Your health might not really be at risk, but often, you'll literally feel it: You're panting. Between meetings, homeschooling, and picking stocks, you ran out of air. You're gasping. So settle down! Sit. Relax. Inhale!

Inhaling is living.

You stare out the window. Nothing moves. Ahhh.

You enjoy the meal that's in front of you. No music. No TV. You can taste every spice. Ahhhhh.

You walk around the block. You see a tree. The leaves are swaying in the wind. "Is it breathing?" you wonder. Ahhhhhhhhhh.

You lie on your back. You stretch your arms and legs into the star that you are. You look at the ceiling. How could you forget to inhale? It's the most natural thing in the world!

Doing is wonderful. Life is a one-time chance to do everything you'll ever do, and I hope most of yours will be a joy to experience. But if do is *all* you do, it'll be impossible to extract happiness from even the most fortunate of events. So don't. Sometimes, just *don't*.

Life is not a vacuum, and so nothingness is not empty. It provides us with the very air we need to witness the full spectrum of the gift we've been given.

Don't forget to inhale.

Part II
Work

"Don't be pushed around by the fears in your mind. Be led by the dreams in your heart."

— *Roy T. Bennet*

The Easiest Job in the World

I'm offering you a job. The salary is more than enough to live comfortably, and, better yet, it consists of only one task: You can't do *anything*.

You can choose whether you'll sit or stand, and you can transition between the two as you please — but that's it. You can't call any friends. You can't listen to music. You can't browse Twitter, write in your diary, or read a book. You can eat and go to the toilet, but you can't run any errands. You can pick your nose, but you can't watch Youtube and definitely no TV.

Oh, and since doing nothing is hard, naturally, this is a full-time job. You'll be required to do nothing for 40 hours each week. How else to ensure your progress? You can't leave early either, by the way.

The big question is: Would you take that job?

———

In the real world, there are many jobs hauntingly similar to the one I just described. Any job where you must "watch something," for example, whether that's a surveillance camera feed, a public swimming pool, or the entrance to a museum, luxury handbag store, or government building. Manning a toll both, punching holes in concert tickets, and "house-sitting" are equally filled with non-activity, as are countless desk jobs both in the private and public sector.

My roommate used to work for our college. Over the course of eight hours, she would send one-line responses to 30 emails, and that was considered a busy day.

When a friend and I returned books to the library, we used to joke that the girl behind the counter had the best job in the world because there was nothing to do. The truth, however, is that her head always lay on her desk as if it weighed a million pounds. She looked out the window with a sense of sadness and longing, clearly wishing to be anywhere but where she was.

Boring jobs are for boring people — but boring people don't exist. Any menial job can only ever be a gateway to something greater. Even the stiffest, most humdrum-seeming bean counter has a reason for cherishing his bean-counting gig. Why? Because the limitedness of his job allows him to be limit*less* somewhere else. Maybe he spends all his energy on his children, reads a book a day, or pushes the boundaries of woodworking in his spare time.

You don't want an easy job. You want a job that allows you to pursue what's meaningful. Sometimes the meaning will come *through* the job, and sometimes it won't — but whenever you can, choose to get paid to learn instead of idling to earn.

Pick a passion project, and then strategically align your work *with it* rather than pitting the two against one another. Maybe you'll have to take a rough job sweeping floors. Perhaps you'll need a prestigious yet unpaid internship with a great mentor. Or, maybe, you'll go for the boring job that affords you plenty of time to read, study, write, learn, code, talk, or connect. Whatever it takes to build something.

Wherever you see your next station in life, doing nothing is never the answer, even if you can get paid for it. Everything has a price, and when it comes to sitting around for too long, it is one even the world's richest person cannot afford — for it'll cost them the only chance they have at living a meaningful life.

For the Jacks

I don't like the phrase "jack of all trades, master of none." First because, in a way, it's true, and I'm the perfect living example. Second because, in today's world, even *when* it's true, its negative implications are upside down. Worst and finally, however, it diminishes the fact that, in order to be a jack of all trades, first, you have to go out and try many things. At least you did something rather than just critique another person's skills.

In the Middle Ages, if you only sort of knew how to repair a horse shoe or weren't quite funny enough to be the king's jester, you were screwed — sometimes literally. In Daniel Defoe's case, the screws were the ones of a pillory, a torture device used to punish criminals by chaining them to a wooden cross in a public place, head and hands exposed.

Curious crowds were then free to sneer and hurl all kinds of insults at the convicted, and not just the ones that hurt psychologically. Beyond rotten eggs, dirt, and dead animals (yes, *dead animals*), riled up mobs would start throwing stones, pans, and other deadly projectiles at the victim. Some criminals died, others suffered lifelong debilitations.

Lucky for Daniel Defoe, it rained heavily during his three pillory sessions, thus minimizing the crowd.[1] Some of the few attendees even brought flowers — a token of appreciation for the very thing that had landed him in shackles. Defoe had written a pamphlet suggesting draconian measures against church dissenters. Being a dissenter himself, the text was meant to be a parody, but unfortunately, no one of importance thought it was funny. Hence the pillory and some time in prison.

When Defoe made it out of jail, the brick factory he used to run was no longer, but he landed a gig at a newspaper and later became a spy for the government. In 1719, he published a book with a little more class. It's a book often considered the first English novel, sparking not just more translations, spin-offs, and adaptations than any other, but an entire literary genre: the "Robinsonade" — the book's title is *Robinson Crusoe*.

Between his brick factory, writing, spy work, investigative journalism, and other pursuits, Defoe seems to me like the epitome of a jack of all trades, which means that, even 300 years ago, you could make a meaningful contribution not *just* through intense focus on one skill. Granted, the further back in time you go, the more will people like Defoe, Da Vinci, Aristotle, and Ada Lovelace mark the exception, not the rule, but the reverse is also true: Today, it often pays *more* than handsomely to be a "jack of all trades, master of junctions," as we might update the phrase for our modern age.

Nowadays, if you know the basics of working a video camera, have a few good inside jokes with friends, and can teach yourself a little editing magic, you might do what Smosh did in 2005: Record funny little sketches and post them on

Youtube. 17 years later, they're still doing it, and their channel now boasts over 25 million subscribers.

Yes, the world will always need specialists, but at some point, most, if not all, specialists will be robots. Once you can teach it how to do it perfectly and reliably, a robot will perform better heart surgery than even the best heart surgeon. A career built on the intersection of a variety of skills might not last forever, but based on combinatorics alone, there's an infinite pool of such careers out there, and you can always pick up a bunch of new skills, *especially* if you're not trying to be world-class at them.

Being a generalist is no longer a bad thing. It is a normal thing. If you're a generalist, polymath, renaissance person, multipotentialite, or whatever colorful term you might call yourself: We need you. We need you and your rainbow of skills and interests.

You might not have written your Robinson Crusoe yet, but you're a jack of all trades, master of junctions — and you're perfect just the way you are.

What Do You Hate Not Doing?

When I don't write, I get angry. I feel it every time I get caught up in other commitments. It's like there's something bottling up inside me. I feel on edge. Anxious. I can only go so long without journaling or writing an article.

According to Derek Sivers, I should lean into that anger. "What do you hate not doing?" he asks in his book *Hell Yeah or No*. "What makes you feel depressed, annoyed, or like your life has gone astray if you don't do it enough?"

If you're trying to find the work you should build your life around, this double-negative question will deliver better ideas than the usual, generic "What makes you happy?" Why? Because *a lot of things* make you happy, most of which aren't work-related to begin with — but even among those that are, you'll likely struggle to pick favorites.

I can find happiness in non-writing tasks, like working on my website. I love analyzing the traffic and optimizing the design. I could also spend hours choosing artwork for my articles, studying the craft, or brainstorming what to write next.

But none of this means I should make any of these activities the main focus of my career.

The truth is if you're a generally positive person, aiming for happiness won't narrow the field enough. You'll always find *some* happiness along the way, no matter what type of work you do. In fact, how happy you are is more a reflection of the habits you've cultivated in your life, like optimism, hope, and humility, than your occupation.

What if, instead of asking yourself what makes you happy, you tuned into what makes you angry? When you're deep in the flow of a design project and someone interrupts you, do you become furious? Do the administrative tasks of being a freelance photographer irritate you, whereas being out there shooting photos makes you feel at peace? Are you sad whenever one of your lectures gets cancelled because you love working with students?

What do you hate not doing?

I shouldn't want to write as much as I do, but that is precisely the point: *I do.* My commitment to writing is irrational. It makes sense neither emotionally nor financially, and yet, if I'm not writing, sooner or later, whatever else I'm doing starts to feel like an annoying barrier keeping me from my true life's work. Find what attracts you beyond reason.

I already knew that writing makes me happy. Now I also know how much *not writing* makes me *unhappy* — and that might be the most valuable lesson of all.

The 3 Fs of Mastery

Practice makes perfect, right? So why is it that countless people practice certain skills for hours on end, but very few ever become world-class? As it turns out, it matters *how* we practice more so than *how much*.

In his book *The Talent Code*, Daniel Coyle discusses "deep practice," a method used by elite musicians, athletes, writers, and other masters of their craft. The idea is that the more new mistakes you can fix in a relatively short period of time, the faster you'll make progress. The emphasis here is on "new." Instead of just repeating both the patterns and mistakes you already know over and over again, aggressively find and fix new faults in your approach. Every time you correct a novel mistake, different combinations of neurons fire in your brain, thus creating the mental pathways that lead to mastery.

Coyle's strategy boils down to three steps. You can use them to practice almost anything more deeply. We can call them "the 3 Fs of mastery:"

1. Fragment it: The easiest way to spot mistakes early is to chop your practice into the smallest sensible unit for your level of proficiency. If you're a piano player, for example, it might make sense to study a new piece one musical bar at a time. If you're a writer, once you have the outline of your book, break individual chapters down further into single paragraphs or even sentences. As a tennis player, you might want to focus exclusively on your serve. Only when you've mastered that particular unit should you move on to the next.

2. Fuse it: Once multiple small parts feel right, you can piece them back together. One paragraph becomes two paragraphs, one page of notes becomes two, and so on. The key is to not over-practice. According to Coyle, many world-class athletes train no more than three to five hours per day. If you do deep practice right, after a certain point, more won't lead to better. It will only lead to exhaustion. "When you depart the deep-practice zone," Coyle writes, "you might as well quit."

3. Feel it: Finally — and this is the difference between professionals and legends — you must learn to "feel it." By absorbing larger, more complex patterns as chains of microscopic, near-self-evident chunks, you'll build a strong gut over time. Eventually, you'll be able to detect anything that "feels off," even if you can no longer pinpoint exactly why an element seems out of place. A writer must be able to read their work and answer the question: "How will it feel from a reader's perspective?" A musician must transcend beyond perfect execution and play in a way only they can play.

Fragment it, fuse it, feel it. Use the 3 Fs of mastery, and become not just good but extraordinary.

Option 1 of 1

I have used hard work to compensate for a lack of knowledge many times. When I wanted to learn how to perform cool soccer tricks, I watched every video I could find and practiced for many hours every day. When I started my blog, I had no idea how to market it. I ran many experiments based on tactics I learned from others, and then I stuck with what worked for me.

I could list countless examples of hard work beating intelligence. I'm sure you'll find plenty in your own life. Common sense says that the more of these examples we look at, the less we'll worry about our intelligence, and the more motivated we'll be to work hard ourselves. To some extent, that's true. On the other hand, you could say that even the most inspiring story doesn't matter. Why? Because hard work is *your only option* anyway.

Let me repeat: Hard work is your *only* option.

If you took an IQ test right now, there would be two possible outcomes. One, you get a result that's below average. Two, you get a result that's above average. Would you change your work ethic in either scenario? Think about it.

Would you work less hard if you found out you were a genius? Would you try any harder if you discovered you weren't? I hope you wouldn't have to. I hope you know that, when you have a goal, your best shot is to do your very best until you get it, regardless of the circumstances.

There's already a great variety of things we don't control: Talent, luck, external events, and, yes, our baseline of intelligence. Dialing the work ethic setting from "lazy" to "persistent" is just about the only thing we *can* control. Why on earth would we make any other choice?

What's more, hard work automatically gets you the best out of all the other levers, even if they're out of reach. The more you use your talent, the better the track record you will build. The more output you create, the more chances at lucky breaks you get. And over time, even the worst circumstances will give way if you keep working.

I don't know what your dream is, but when you really commit yourself to it, only only one of two things can happen. Either one day, after many years of work and endless wins and losses, you will achieve your dream, or you will die trying along the way — with zero regrets that you gave it your all.

The only other option? To give up. To quit. To look at your dream and say, "You're not worth it. You're too hard. I can't chase you. I'm not strong enough." Well, you *are* strong enough, and if you ask me, giving up is not an alternative. Not on your dream. We only get one life.

No matter how intelligent you are, there'll always be infinitely more to know than you already do, but whether you decide to work on a Sunday, stay after practice ends, or tend to your garden after dark, that's up to you.

Choose hard work. Choose hard work either way.

Don't 80/20 Your Dream

If you use the 80/20 rule on everything, you'll live an unsatisfying life.

Ironically, economist Vilfredo Pareto only discovered this seemingly universal principle — that 20% of the input usually accounts for 80% of the output — *because* he outright ignored it. Pareto didn't just track the output of his vegetable garden. He was obsessed with it. The man counted peas in spreadsheets, for God's sake — in 1896!

Eventually, Pareto noticed that a small share of his pods held a large number of the overall peas, a pattern of distribution he then applied to land ownership in Italy.[1] When the logic held up, he became famous, and today, the principle named after him can be found everywhere.

Vilfredo Pareto put no less than 100% of his energy into a mundane, seemingly meaningless hobby, and it led to a breakthrough at his job. Those are the facts, and we must not confuse them with the fictions now surrounding his idea. Instead of "settle for doing one fifth of the job," the lesson here is this: If you don't give your best *somewhere*, you'll never get to the top of anything — or, as in Pareto's case, the bottom of it.

If you only do 20% of the work, you'll only get 20% of the satisfaction, regardless of the outcome. Humans aren't designed for half-assery. Will we get away with doing just the minimum on *some* days? Sure. But not *every day*, if only for the fact that your brain will start eating itself alive. We max out at 100%, and, more often than not, we need to use every last bit of our wits to feel fulfilled.

If you never try your hardest, you'll never know what you're capable of. Sure, you'll get the comfort of "I only failed because I didn't try," but that won't last long before it decomposes into regret.

The 80/20 principle is a fantastic approach for everything you don't really care about. If you walk ten minutes away from the airport before calling an Uber, you'll save 20% on the fare. Good! It is better to exercise for ten minutes a day than to not exercise at all. Great! But if your finances, your career, or your health means everything to you, you don't want to take the easy way out. You want to go all-in *and* go all the way.

If you want to write a bestseller, 20% won't cut it. If you want to make millions, 20% won't cut it. If you want to be the best dad in the world, 20% won't cut it.

Tim Ferriss wrote about the Pareto principle in *The 4-Hour Workweek*. The book was Tim's template for automating a company he had built but no longer cared about. In writing it, however, he left nothing to chance. He engineered *every* aspect of the book, and that's why it became such a hit.

When you find your unique path to greatness, walk on it, and walk all the way.

You don't always have to exert yourself, of course, and yes, sometimes you'll give 100% in an area that might not be the most relevant. You never know, however, when and where you might reap the fruits of your labor — but unless you cultivate a garden, you can't harvest anything at all.

If you don't go all-in somewhere, some of the time, you'll never feel the magic the 80/20 rule promises but fails to deliver: "Today I did my very best, and that was enough."

Working on What Matters

You either work on what matters, or you work on what doesn't. There is nothing in-between.

Sometimes, we choose the unimportant because someone else told us to. Sometimes, we lack the energy, physical or mental. Most of the time, however, we do it because we're scared.

In our modern world, fear seldom shows us what's dangerous. It shows us what matters. Once you're a proficient writer, it's easy to churn out more articles. It's scary to resist publishing in order to write a book. The fear shows you where the growth is: Repeat yourself forever, or work on bigger things.

It doesn't matter whether you send emails, juggle numbers, coordinate people, or ship projects. There's always one that's important and another one that isn't.

Pick the important. And if you can't get rid of the fear, remember that, as Emma Donoghue said, "scared is what you're feeling," but "brave is what you're doing."

The Most Valuable Skill in the World

Charles Proteus Steinmetz was an early-20th-century mathematician and electrical engineer who helped develop the alternating current electricity that comes out of the power sockets in your house today.

Born as Carl August Ruldoph Steinmetz in Germany, Charles aptly chose his new middle name when he emigrated to the United States in 1889: In Greek mythology, Proteus is an all-knowing, shapeshifting sea god, his real form being an old man with a hunchback. Steinmetz too was a genius, but he also suffered from dwarfism and other deformities, standing just four feet tall.

Besides holding over 200 patents at the time of his death and counting people like Albert Einstein and Nikola Tesla among his peers, Steinmetz solved countless issues standing in the way of electricity appearing wherever it was needed. One such issue plagued Henry Ford in the early 1920s.

During the construction of Ford's new River Rouge automotive plant, a massive generator kept failing. Steinmetz was called in to help, and when he appeared on the premises, he asked for nothing but pen and paper, a bed, and to be left alone. Smithsonian Mag recounts what happened next:[1]

> *Steinmetz listened to the generator and scribbled computations on the notepad for two straight days and nights. On the second night, he asked for a ladder, climbed up the generator and made a chalk mark on its side. Then he told Ford's skeptical engineers to remove a plate at the mark and replace sixteen windings from the field coil. They did, and the generator performed to perfection.*
>
> *Henry Ford was thrilled — until he got an invoice from General Electric in the amount of $10,000. Ford acknowledged Steinmetz's success but balked at the figure. He asked for an itemized bill. Steinmetz responded personally to Ford's request with the following:*
>
> *Making chalk mark on generator: $1.*
>
> *Knowing where to make mark: $9,999.*
>
> *Ford paid the bill.*

There's a lot to be learned from this story about patience, diligence, and knowing your value. There's a lesson in there about accepting help once you've asked for it, and one about the blasphemy of paying people by the hour, but the biggest one, by far, is this: Good judgement is the most valuable skill in the world.

It's true that great judgement will make you rich. After all, $10,000 in 1920 equates to more than $500,000 in wages today,[2] and that's just for production workers, not even someone as skilled as Steinmetz. Not bad for two days' work.

More importantly, however, you'll need accurate judgement

to live a happy life. Deciding who you trust requires judgement. Choosing who you marry is a judgement call. And how you spend your time is a direct result of your judgement.

Steinmetz, for example, wanted nothing more than to raise a family. Afraid to pass on his disease, however, he decided not to marry. Instead, he arranged for a coworker and his wife to live in his mansion, and he later even became the "grandfather" of their three children. It takes judgement both to know yourself and to build your life around said self-awareness.

Since judgement is so valuable, nature made it hard to get: The only way to good judgement leads through experience which, in turn, you must pay for with time, energy, and by taking risks. Ironically, even more so than all the other factors, you'll need courage.

Life may be one big judgement training camp, but in order to get the most out of it, you must face your most important decision, choose an option, and then see it through — over and over again. Like asking a colleague to move in with you, sending a big invoice, or telling someone twice your size what to do, that's not a matter of judgement at all. It is a question of courage. Be brave like Charles Proteus Steinmetz.

Public Speaking for the Rest of Us

In 1975, Ray Dalio founded an investment company out of his apartment. Nearly 50 years later, Bridgewater Associates is the largest hedge fund in the world, managing over 150 billion dollars for their clients. Along the way, Ray has learned how to lead over 1,500 people and how to read the economy like an open book. He has also mastered navigating the ranks of the most powerful people on the planet, to which, as one of the 100 richest people in the world, Ray now belongs.

30 seconds into Ray's TED talk, however, you'll spot something that doesn't fit that description of him at all: Scribbled onto the middle and ring finger of his left hand is a cheat sheet — because Ray is nervous. Other signs will appear throughout the talk: Ray is shaking lightly, his voice sometimes breaks, and he occasionally suffers from dry mouth syndrome.

Ray Dalio is an introvert. His inward focus might be the source of his achievements, but it also means he doesn't like the spotlight. Never has, never will. Therefore, despite countless public appearances, at over 70 years old, Ray is still afraid of public speaking — but he also knows some things are too important to let fear bury them. He once told Business Insider that "while he knew that making himself more public would be difficult for him, he was faced with a choice to either work through his fear and share his message, or let his principles be analyzed without his input."[1]

Before his first TV interview in 1978, Steve Jobs said he was "ready to throw up at any moment."[2] In *The War of Art*, Steven Pressfield recounts that famous actor Henry Fonda was "still throwing up before each stage performance, even when he was 75. In other words, fear doesn't go away."

Only very few people are born to be on stage. The rest of us, even *the best of us*, are stuck being Ray Dalio. The fear will never go away.

The best thing we can do is take comfort in the fact that we're not alone, find our courage, and ask ourselves the same question even a man as accomplished as Ray asks himself before each public appearance: "When you have discomfort, do you let discomfort stand in the way of doing what you think is the right thing?"

Seneca's LinkedIn

If Lucius Annaeus Seneca, one of ancient Rome's premier Stoic philosophers, had had a LinkedIn profile, I dare guess which motto he'd have included in his introduction.

As children, we rarely question whether the fun thing to do is also the *right* thing to do, and, to be fair, most of the time, there really is no difference. Why *wouldn't* a child play soccer all day long, make up stories in her mind, or build sandcastles with friends?

It is only once we grow up that we assume honor and pleasure must always be in stark opposition. But just because our definitions of "fun" and "right" change, that does not mean the two are no longer compatible. In fact, finding the activities in your life that unite them is the whole point.

For me, writing is a pleasure. I enjoy it so much, I would do it for free. Often, that's exactly what ends up happening. However, I am still honored to get paid for it some of the time. Enough to keep doing it, even. It is also humbling that thousands of people will earnestly consider what I have to say.

It makes me choose my words carefully, including the ones you are reading right now.

Pleasurable work makes you look forward to waking up every morning. You'll jump out of bed, eager for another round of wrestling with your favorite opponent, whether it's project management, UX design, or playing the violin. Pleasure lets us tackle our tasks with joy and vigor.

Honorable work makes you accountable. Once you start practicing your art in public, you'll build an audience. Your team at work depends on you. Regardless of the specifics, as soon as other people become involved, you'll feel a natural urge to do your work responsibly. Honor preserves your humility, and it gives you the courage to make difficult decisions.

When I updated my LinkedIn after years of inactivity, I found a quote staring back at me from the bottom of my introduction. It made me smile. It's been there for as long as I've had my profile, and it just might be the only element I'll never change:

> *"Reach that destination where the things that are pleasant and the things that are honorable finally become, for you, the same."*
>
> — *Lucius Annaeus Seneca*

Human Communication 101

Good communication is always simple. What's hard is having the courage to let it be. To say "I don't love you," rather than concoct some elaborate web of intricate, lesser truths — or even outright lies — hoping the other will stumble into it, trip, and fall over all on their own.

In the movie *Hitch*, communication expert Alex Hitchens claims that "60% of all human communication is nonverbal: body language. 30% is your tone. So that means 90% of what you're saying ain't coming out of your mouth." It sounds intriguing, but it grossly underestimates the importance of truth. If you've ever sheepishly confessed something, you know: A powerful sentence uttered poorly may be weaker than it could be, but it doesn't turn the truth into a lie. People can tell what we tell, and they'll react accordingly.

When I fail to communicate clearly, it's rarely because of complex circumstances. It's that I'm too afraid to say what I truly think and believe. As such, I have wiggled my way around questions, said "yes" when I meant to say "no," shied away from asking for help, and hated saying "sorry." I did all of this in hopes of the truth magically finding its way to the light, which, of course, it never does — because it's *my* job to take it there. *The* job, really. A job for all of us.

I'm not sure how much of what we're saying comes out of our mouths, but I know that 90% of what does is a weak version of the truth. We may soften it to be polite, censor ourselves to maintain our image, or ask for less than we want because it's more than we think we deserve, but at the root of it all, there'll always be fear. I can't hand you the power to act in spite of this fear. It's a war fought in countless battles over one's lifetime. What I *can* do, however, is give you a little vial full of useful truths to keep at hand. This one contains seven of them. Here's hoping you and I will use them more often in the future.

1. When you don't know something, say, "I don't know." People will respect you for it.
2. When you don't understand something, say, "I don't understand." People will explain again.
3. When you don't agree with something, say, "I don't agree." People will accept your opinion.
4. When you don't want to do something, say, "I don't want to do this." People will find a way without you.
5. When you struggle with going it alone, say, "Please help me with this." People will give you a hand.
6. When you like someone, say, "I like you." People will like you back.
7. When you know you did something wrong, say, "I'm sorry. That was my fault." People will forgive you.

After you find the courage to speak one of these lines, always leave room for one more thing: listening. The following communication expert didn't have as much research as Hitch to back up his statistics, but then again, the numbers of nature never lie:

> *"We have two ears and one mouth so we may listen twice as much as we speak."*
>
> — *Epictetus*

Perseverance

The irony of "date doctor" Alex Hitchens' methods is that they work for everyone but himself. When "Hitch," played by Will Smith in the eponymous movie, tries to woo journalist Sara Melas, he keeps making a fool of himself. Unable to secure her phone number, he sends a walkie-talkie to her office and, in his first message, asks her whether she knows the definition of perseverance:

"Continuing a course of action without regard to discouragement, opposition, or previous failure."

For the rest of the movie, Hitch will indeed keep going from failure to failure before Sara finally allows him into her heart. This is the typical, obstacle-based view of perseverance most of us are familiar with.

When he spoke at Hustle Con in 2017, however, Casey Neistat struck a different tone. The host asked Casey, "What was your biggest failure?" Immediately, Casey responded: "The biggest failure was celebrating success." It's a point Casey has made time and again: "With every success should come a bigger, more ambitious goal. It took a couple of years I would describe as 'failure' to be able to appreciate that."

Now, Casey isn't telling us to keep chasing success because he's greedy or delusional or an egomaniac. In his vlog celebrating his growth from 500,000 to four million subscribers in just 18 months,[1] he explains: "The moment you're born, you start barreling towards the only finish line [in life], which is death. And no matter what you do, this momentum can never be slowed, and it can never stop."

Therefore, Casey asserts, "life is about movement; life is a trajectory; life is a train that never stops" — and so is his career. Considering his work a never-ending string of little failures and successes, Casey sees the wins as equally obstructive to perseverance as others might see discouragement, opposition, or failure. "Today's success quickly becomes yesterday's success, becomes last week's success, becomes last year's success."

Einstein died when he was 76 years old. In his last week, he finished a manifesto, prepared a radio speech, and by his deathbed, his family members found 12 pages full of equations. Einstein didn't frantically try to remedy some previous failure or achieve something new to cement his legacy. Like Casey, he just wasn't done — and he knew he never would be.

Both of them embody a 2,000-year-old piece of advice from Marcus Aurelius: "Receive without pride, let go without attachment." In *The Daily Stoic*, Ryan Holiday explains why we should treat failure and success exactly the same way: "Do not take the slights of the day personally — or the exciting rewards and recognitions either, especially when duty has assigned you an important cause. Trivial details like the rise and fall of your position say nothing about you as a person. Only your behavior will."

Failure and success are external events. Like seasons, they come and they go. So let them! Neither one must define you.

Piece all of the above perspectives together, and you get a new, more appropriate definition of perseverance:

> *"Continuing a course of action without regard to discouragement, **encouragement**, opposition, **support**, previous failure, or **previous success**."*

That's the kind of perseverance we want. The kind that lasts a lifetime, and that'll carry us through both the ups *and* the downs on the journey between life and death. Regardless of whether it lands us an Emmy, a date, or a promotion, if this is the attitude that gets one to excitedly take notes on their deathbed, then, to me, that is success.

Part III
(Tough) Love

"A friend is someone who knows all about you and still loves you."

— *Elbert Hubbard*

If You Want the Zig, Accept the Zag

Life isn't fair, and that's a good thing. Volatility is your friend because volatility means change, and only if there is a capacity for *change* can there be a capacity for *growth*.

Often, we don't want the volatility because we fear the change will be negative. What we miss is that by wishing for stability, we also wish life would limit our potential — and that's not a sensible thing to wish for.

Rarely in life can you have it both ways, and while it's natural to focus on protecting your downside, it's easy to forget the upside altogether, and yet, the *potential* for upside is always there.

Let's say you're a Youtuber, and, from one month to the next, your views drop by 50%. That's alarming, and so the alarm bells you ring, both in private and in public. You complain to Youtube. You worry every day. You wish "things would just go back to normal." But what if your views had doubled?

In that case, you wouldn't be complaining. You'd be celebrating. You'd announce on social media how proud you are, and how long and hard you've worked to deserve this. You wouldn't message Youtube and thank them. You would believe you had earned this success, and you'd be right — but you can't have it both ways.

You could replace this example with a million others, and they'd all highlight the same truth: You want the zig but not the zag, and that's just a crooked perspective on how the world works. The zig and the zag only travel together, so if we want either one, we *must* accept them both.

If your views didn't have the potential to fall 50%, they also wouldn't have the potential to double. You hate it when they dip and love it when they grow, but the possibility of *both* must exist for either one of them to happen.

This is a principle of life. It's like gravity. You can't negotiate your way out of it. Sometimes, you can twist the odds slightly in your favor, but in the grand scheme of things, there is no way to eliminate all the risk without eliminating all the rewards.

A secure job where your income will double in a year? You want the zig but not the zag.

A stable relationship with few obligations? You want the zig but not the zag.

A high-growth portfolio with steady returns? You want the zig but not the zag.

Life is not a straight line, and that's one of the best things about it. Stop trying to have it both ways so you can accept what's always been true: There will be highs, there will be lows, but if you embrace them both, they'll carry you beyond your wildest dreams in a never-ending cycle.

Accept or Convince

Accept or convince. Those are your two choices. Often, we insist on convincing when, usually, accepting is not just easier, it is also the right thing to do.

Munich is a city of cyclists. Students cycle. Athletes cycle. Even consultants cycle. I don't like cycling. Too many accidents. Too much trauma. It never grew on me. Yet people insist on convincing me to cycle.

"It's so much faster! It's easy! You can rent bikes with an app! Your life would be so much better!" Actually, my life is better for never having to think any of these thoughts.

I also never have to worry about where I'll park my bike. I never forget where I put it. I don't get honked at by furious car drivers in traffic, and I never fall off my bike. I don't need a helmet, tire pump, or replacement tubes. I never have to wonder whether I locked my bike, whether someone might steal it, or how much the bill for repairing it will be.

The world always wants to sell you on how great it would be to have this new thing in your life. Or that one. Or that one. It never tells you how fantastic it feels to eliminate an entire area, including all purchases, items, habits, behaviors, and even thoughts associated with it.

Convincing requires a lot of effort because it only happens once, but when it does, it might drag an entire lifetime of maintenance work into your little world. Acceptance is free. It is effortless. You can do it all day long, with many people, and as many times as you like.

It's natural to be excited about new experiences. To want to share them and invite others to join you. What's not natural is pushing your opinion so hard on someone that they fall over because of it, especially when they seem perfectly content without it. Nor is it normal to give in to that pressure when you're on the receiving end of it.

Demand acceptance if you must, and remember: You can't make someone happier by talking them into the exact thing they are glad to be rid of.

Accept or convince — which one will you choose?

Happiness Is Third Grade Math

James Altucher says happiness is third grade math:[1] All you have to do is divide your reality by your expectations.

In a fraction, when the denominator outgrows the numerator, the result falls below 1 and moves towards 0. Similarly, when your expectations grow far beyond your reality, your happiness goes to zero.

Let's say you come home and find a big, unexpected gift on your doorstep. A handbag perhaps or a new gaming console. Your reality skyrockets. You had no expectations. Your happiness goes through the roof!

Now imagine you spill your coffee as you sit down to work. The numerator decreases. Reality threw a curveball. You didn't expect stains on your desk today, so the denominator is still the same — and your happiness goes down.

We can't control our reality, but we can change our expectations. That's the only "trick" there is. Whenever your reality fails you, *immediately* adjust your expectations. This is the one lever you can truly pull, and with some practice, you can pull it within seconds each time.

As your coffee races towards your stack of notes, shift your expectations from "I'll have a productive start to my day" to "I'll have a nice, shiny desk when I'm done cleaning this up." When your software won't send the email, go from "I'll be out of here in five minutes" to "I'll feel relieved once I close my laptop for the day." If your partner breaks up with you, go from "I'll never have to worry about dating again" to "I'll learn something from this situation."

Like that last one, not all of these shifts are easy to make. Some will take years to fully embrace, but you can *start* all of them in a matter of seconds — and many you can finish just as quickly. Sure, a breakup is something to chew on, but spilling your coffee? Tech problems? You won't even remember those next week, so there's no point in spoiling your happiness over them today.

Making these micro-shifts won't turn you into a doormat. You can still expect others to treat you well. You also needn't lower your aspirations, just let go of the artificial timelines you've constructed for them. Patience, flexibility, and a balanced life — these are the rewards for adjusting your expectations whenever reality changes.

A perpetual state of low expectations sounds nice in theory. If they were always at zero, nearly everything would be a pleasant surprise, and even bad news would hurt a lot less. That's an ideal we can strive towards, but it's unlikely we'll ever reach it. For now, let's do what we can with what we've got.

Whenever your reality falls short of your expectations, immediately adjust. Direct your vision to a new five-minute future. How can you course-correct *right now?* How can you shift the formula based on your current situation? Practice, practice, practice.

Your expectations only add to your happiness insofar as they fall short of your reality. You can't prevent the world from turning against you on occasion, but you can ensure your expectations never trail far behind.

Happiness really is like third-grade math: We can figure out most problems quickly, but if we want lifelong mastery, we must solve a few equations each day.

You Don't Need a New Thing to Be Grateful For

Every night, I write down three things I'm grateful for. I've been doing this for ten years. That's more than 10,000 voluntary thank-yous. At first, I tried hard to be creative. "What did I not write down yet? What's something unique to be grateful for?"

James Altucher is big on this. He calls it "difficult gratitude":[1] "When stuck in traffic, be grateful to be living in such a magnificent place that everyone wants to be there. When a child yells back, see the birth of independence of yet another unique personality beginning its private journey on this planet."

In the beginning, it was easy to come up with a great variety of things. As it always does, however, eventually, life happened. I got lazy. Busy. I had bad days. When I felt tired, I just threw together three quick things. When I was sad or unmotivated, I listed the same stuff.

Initially, I felt bad whenever I repeated a previous reason. "I'm not as grateful as I should be. If I was more grateful, I'd find better things," I told myself. One day, however, I realized: Gratitude is not a creativity exercise. It's a gratitude exercise.

You don't need a new thing to be grateful for each day. You need to understand it's the *same* things, over and over again, that make you happy. Don't feel bad for covering the basics. After all, the basics are what matters.

At least 200 of my thank-yous went to coffee. You might say that's boring, but I find it reassuring. How comforting if, time and again, you realize all you need is coffee, cheap groceries, and free music on Youtube to have a good day.

If you need a new gratitude fix every day, if you chase ever bigger outcomes in hopes of putting them on that list, you're doing it wrong. Gratitude is not a game of ambition. That's the *opposite* of what it's for.

Sometimes, I still try to be creative. Instead of coffee itself, I might pick my coffee *maker*, which, despite also counting ten years, hasn't broken down yet. But whenever I catch myself writing down another thing I've used a thousand times, I smile.

A warm bed, free wifi, fresh air. These are the things that make life an honor to wake up to, not winning an Oscar or seeing the pyramids. Those are just the gravy — and we all know fries taste best with ketchup.

Pericles

In the Peloponnesian War, general Pericles led 100 ships into battle. As they charged towards the enemy, a solar eclipse shrouded the world in darkness. Unaware of the science behind the event, panic broke out among the soldiers.

Pericles took off his coat, walked to the navigator, and held it around his head. "Are you afraid of what you see?" "Of course not," the navigator said, "this is just a piece of black cloth!" Pericles removed the coat and looked at the navigator: "Then what does it matter if the cause of darkness is a different one?"

When we don't understand life, we tend to imagine worst-case scenarios. The result is fear, and fear leads to bad decisions. What if, instead, we tried adjusting our perspective? Perspective is everything, and we are free to change ours at every second.

We can judge any situation from many angles. We can break it down into its parts. We have the option of looking *at* it, past it, into it, around it, or even through it. However many perspectives we must try, eventually, we will find one that allows us to move forward — and that's the whole point of living.

The purpose of thought experiments isn't to provide you with answers to individual perspective problems. It is to give you the courage to face the unknown. Often, it only takes a minute to find this courage, and you can use a single story, like Pericles and the solar eclipse, to stay calm in rough waters.

Don't let your imagination spiral into fear. Take a breath, pause, and then flip through different points of view until you find one that works. Explain the fear away and realize: The cause of darkness doesn't matter. What matters is that we go on.

The Secret

458 essays, 481 book summaries, and 409 articles. Add to that countless mini projects, ebooks, guest posts, web pages, and emails, and what do you get?

You get five million views here, eight million views there, 30 million in another place, and everything that comes with it: A million readers. A big email list. Enough money to keep doing it, and the joy of waking up to this realization every single day.

That's it. That's all there is. That is the secret. From Seth Godin's 7,000th blog post:[1] "The secret to writing a daily blog is to write every day. And to queue it up and blog it. There is no other secret."

Sometimes he thinks he writes his books to promote the blog, not vice versa, Seth says. Sometimes there are typos. But none of these modalities matter. What matters is this: "I write every word. I don't understand outsourcing something this personal, a privilege this important."

My entrepreneur friends are excited to hand off creative work. I'm not. I did exactly one ghostwriting gig in my life. I hated it. Not having my name on something I had written felt like losing a limb.

Sharing your art is a privilege. An act of service. The honors should be attached to your name, and so should the fallout. That's how you learn.

Your art can take infinite forms, from singing to being a parent to project management, but the only way to grow is to learn and share every day. You will forget many lessons, receive others twice, and have to unlearn what you've mastered when life's current changes. But the people loyal to you, your contribution, and your commitment? They'll follow you all the way.

Your journey is cumulative, but only if you take it in public. There is no substitute. It has to be you. *You* have to be there. *You* have to show up every day.

There is nothing else to it, and there never will be. That is the secret.

2 Kinds of Comfort

There are two kinds of comfort. One is a deep-seated, emotional conviction that, no matter what happens, life will be okay. The other is the warm, pleasant feeling you get when you lie snug in your bed. It's called "comforter" for a reason.

Comfort as in "conviction" is crucial to living authentically. Without it, we can't weather the barrage of obstacles, dismissal, and emotional difficulties en route to our dreams.

Comfort as in "convenience," be it physical or emotional, may just be the single-biggest, self-erected stumbling block on our path.

In a world where Amazon, McDonalds, Netflix, Spotify, AirBnB, Uber, and Tinder provide everything at a single fingertap, no one wants to do things the hard way. Why give up comfort now for happiness later? Everything in life should be cheap, fast, and easy. Cheap, fast, easy.

There is only one problem: Nothing worth having comes cheap. Nothing worth having comes fast. And nothing worth having comes easy.

If you're not willing to walk, you'll never run a marathon.
If you're not willing to work out, you'll never be fit.
If you're not willing to cook, you'll never eat healthily.
If you're not willing to travel, you'll never go places.
If you're not willing to go on a date, you'll never find love.
If you're not willing to turn off the TV, you'll never read.
If you're not willing to write, you'll never publish a book.
If you're not willing to press publish, you'll never know if you're any good.
If you're not willing to show yourself on camera, you'll never become a Youtuber.
If you're not willing to practice the piano, you'll never give a concert.
If you're not willing to wear old shoes, you'll never be able to afford new ones.
If you're not willing to sit on the floor, you'll never deserve your own office.
If you're not willing to work on your hobby, you'll never make money the way you want to.
If you're not willing to save money, you'll never have peace of mind.
If you're not willing to invest, you'll never be rich.
If you're not willing to wake up, you'll never make your dreams a reality.
If you're not willing to stay convinced while giving up convenience, to find comfort in being uncomfortable, you'll never live the life you want.

Don't Wait

If you want to learn the piano, press one key today. If you want to write a book, write one paragraph today. If you want a better relationship, make one confession today.

Whatever you do, don't wait. Don't wait for tomorrow. Not again. Not now. It's time. Take the gloves off. This is it. One life, one time. No do overs. Don't wait.

If you want a new job, learn one new thing today. If you want a big money cushion, save $1 today. If you want to feel inspired, study one of your heroes today.

Objects can't move without momentum. You have to *be* in motion to *stay* in motion. It doesn't matter how small the push. It only matters that it's there.

Imperceptible growth now leads to exponential growth later. *Trust* the imperceptible. Do the small things first. Do what feels ridiculous. You must crawl before you can run, but you *must not wait*.

If you want to run a marathon, run for ten minutes today. If you want to be a chef, make scrambled eggs today. If you want to teach children, help one child today.

Urgency isn't coming. No one will kick your butt in gear. Urgency isn't the postman. You can't rely on it to show up each day. But if you're already checking the door, you might as well go for a run. *You* show up each day.

You must be the one to bring the urgency. *You* must understand that life is finite. *You* have to allow for that to click. And you have to do that *today*.

If you want to start a business, send one email today. If you want to make friends, ask one person to coffee today. If you want to be a thought leader, post one idea today.

Regret is a sneaky bastard. Always late to the party. When regret shows up, it's time to go home. Too late already. "Nothing to see here folks, just another human on a trip down misery lane." Ugh. You again. Regret. Jackass.

If you want to read a book, read one page today. If you want to paint a landscape, make one stroke today. If you want to bury the hatchet, call one relative today.

The river of time carries all of us away. Redemption makes for a nice story, but it's not guaranteed. The only promise you have is today. Don't wait. Use today.

If you want to find freedom, choose peace of mind today. If you want to make history, take a stand today. If you want to be a better human, change one behavior today.

Whatever you do, don't wait. Don't wait for tomorrow. Not again. Don't wait.

How You Do Anything Is How You Do Everything

There are only two ways to look at the world: One is that nothing matters. The other is that everything does. Both are true.

On the one hand, you'll likely be forgotten soon after you're gone. On the other hand, it's impossible to tell how your actions will add up. Who knows? 100 years from now, they might make a huge difference for the world.

Which of these worldviews you choose is up to you, but only one affords you a real chance at finding meaning and happiness. Personally, I'd pick optimism any time — but there's a catch: If everything matters, you can never weasel out of responsibility. Ever.

Consequences have consequences. Everything you do is a domino, kicking off an infinite chain of endlessly evolving events as it falls. Therefore, how you do even the smallest of things will determine how that sequence unfolds. In other words: How you do anything is how you do everything.

In one study room at my college, the door is quite heavy. You have to press the handle properly for it to shut. I have watched dozens of people enter and leave that room, and I have yet to see a single person after whom it won't swing wide open. It's as if an entire generation was never taught how to manually close a door with care. *With care.* That is the point. How you do anything is how you do everything.

The only way to write a book is to start with one page, one paragraph, one sentence. The only way to make a million is to make a dollar. And the only way to be loved is to begin to be loving.

Life is big, but it consists of many small moments. The only way to do great things is to chain together countless of these moments into one brilliant, shiny sequence. To keep toppling dominoes. As a corollary, it makes no sense to do the small things wrong just because they're small — especially if the opposite leads to greatness. How you do anything is how you do everything.

So close the door. Do it right. And remember that everything matters.

On Taking the Stairs

When there's a set of stairs with an escalator next to it, which option do you choose? It feels like a small, near-irrelevant decision, but actually, it's a bigger deal than you think. Behind this tiny, seemingly innocuous choice — do you walk or do you stand? — lies a whole way of looking at the world.

In contrast to their stair-climbing counterparts, the people on the escalator lose time, momentum, and energy. They choose to slow down when they could keep their pace, to stop when they could be moving. In other words, they choose to wait when they could choose to do something.

Not that doing something is always the answer. Sometimes, it is absolutely time to wait. To rest. To take a moment to think. Most of the people on the escalator, however, don't stand because it makes sense to stand *right now*. They stand because it's their *default* to stand. To wait.

Even if they're unaware of it, most people take the escalator because they subconsciously hope the world will magically carry them where they want to go. In this case literally. Unfortunately, the escalator at the airport, the train station, or the shopping mall is just about the only scenario in life where that actually works.

Meanwhile, the people taking the stairs know that every minute counts. They see a staircase leading up a mountain and say, "Okay, bring it on!" They take the obstacle head on and do what they can to overcome it. Instead of losing momentum, they build more. They charge, and their metabolism kicks in.

Life is neither black nor white. When you need a break, take a break. When you're busy rushing through the city, enjoy a moment of quiet with your partner. Slow down if you want to assess the challenge ahead, weigh your options carefully, or form a plan of action — but the question still remains: What is your default?

Even if you do your very best, you might not get what you want. So actually, your very best is the least you can do.

Zig Ziglar once said: "There is no elevator to success. You have to take the stairs."[1] It's cheesy, but it's true. There is also no escalator, and if there was, it would be going the wrong way. You'd have to *run* to get to the top.

Casey Neistat put it like this: "Life is like going the wrong way on a moving sidewalk. Walk, and you stay put. Stand still, and you go backwards. You have to hustle to get ahead."[2]

Taking the stairs instead of the escalator may seem like a silly little decision, but make a silly little decision a thousand times, and it begins to add up — first to a pattern, then to a habit, and ultimately to a belief you hold with all your heart.

Take the stairs, not the escalator. Sure, the extra exercise is nice, but the mindset of being a doer? That will last forever.

2-Minute Pep Talks

Why Birds Fly

On my daily walk, I once saw two birds sitting on a power line. Resting. Chatting. After a brief exchange, they hopped further apart on the line. They glanced at each other a few times, then let themselves fall — and with one powerful spread of their wings, each went their own way.

That's what birds do: They fly. And even though they can fall *from* the sky just once, every morning, they decide to take the leap regardless.

Once a bird is in the air, it soars. Everything flows. The world passes by. Life is a dream, an adventure. The journey it's meant to be. But every time a bird takes off, before it plunges from the power line, there's the risk that, this time, it might fall.

Fitness coach Jerzy Gregorek has a saying: "Hard choices, easy life. Easy choices, hard life."

Even if you know you can, *deciding* to fly is a hard choice. It must be made over and over again, but every time you do, you'll get that weightless feeling, and life will become a little easier.

What's the alternative, really? Doing nothing? Humans can't

stay in their nest. We must take the leap. Take off. Life looks better from above. True living happens when we fly.

Whatever you do today, whether it's resting, chatting, exploring, working, or letting life's current carry you where it may, remember that, soon, you'll have to fall again. When that time comes, don't fret. Don't hesitate. Don't wish it was easier. Just leap. Leap and spread your wings.

You weren't made to sit around. You were born to fly.

Gossip Girl 1813

Bridgerton is a period drama set against the backdrop of London's high society in the early 19th century. Think *Gossip Girl* 200 years ago. The characters' challenges are remarkably similar to what we might call "first-world problems" today: None of them suffer from a lack of food or shelter, but they all struggle with questions of meaning and happiness, particularly those around expectations.

Daphne wants to marry for love, not status, but she doesn't get to pick her perfect match. So does Anthony who, despite being afforded more freedoms than his sister, also finds the woman he loves off limits due to her societal standing. Colin does not feel ready to get married at all, and Eloise would rather travel the world alone than drink tea with some lord.

As the Bridgertons shuffle from event to event, the show's theme emerges: Everyone is watching. At every ball, summer fest, and gala dinner, they're *all* always watching. The queen. The neighbors. The servants. From the doorman to the grandfather, from the gentleman to the clumsy suitor, and from the youngest daughter to the most respectable widow, everyone is constantly observing everyone else, looking for clues, waiting for an attack, ready to parry.

The aim, of course, is to paralyze every participant by mere means of staring. That's why the judging eyes of society never close: If everyone's gaze is locked on someone else, no one is free to move. Like pawns glued to a chessboard, each piece remains in place, and the status quo is preserved.

Unfortunately, every chess piece is a human — a person full of dreams, desires, and ambitions, at least some of which won't conform to society's preconceived notions — and, in the long run, it is impossible for humans not to move.

The result of this silent game of cat and mouse is that every member of "the ton" is anxious. Families prepare big events under great stress. Who to invite? Who to seat next to whom? Separated lovers cry into their pillows, and business deals are struck in hidden chambers. That seems to be the only place where the Bridgertons can find some relief: in secret.

When Benedict, who wishes to be an artist instead of a businessman, attends the party of a painter who lives the life he longs for, he discovers his idol is gay. He later confronts his mentor, and the true artist calls out the comfortable nobleman: "I risk my life every day for love. It takes courage to live outside the traditional expectations of society. You talk of doing the same. But perhaps it is merely just that. All talk."

As recently as 200 years ago, summoning said courage often meant risking death, be it by breaking the law or ending up ostracized. Today, we are lucky. Defying society seldom leads us to the brink, but it requires courage all the same. The courage to turn off Twitter. The courage to share something vulnerable. The courage to embrace who you are.

In 48 BC, Julius Caesar "dated" Cleopatra. A Roman dictator in liaison with a disempowered Egyptian queen — can you imagine the scandal? Spitting in the face of Caesar's childless marriage in Rome, the two even had a son, Caesarion. Caesar never acknowledged him in public and, in his will, declared his grandnephew Octavian as his heir. Cleopatra, however, repeatedly spoke up. She never denied the truth and demanded Caesarion be given his rightful place, which, as the last pharaoh of ancient Egypt, he eventually was.

You and I can't fathom what it was like to live during the Bridgertons' or Caesar's times, but we can let the examples of those choosing courage over compliance inspire us. Be it 48 BC, 1813, or 2022, judging eyes will always be upon us — let's not give a damn about society's expectations.

Reunion

It's prom night. Finally! High school graduation is upon John and his friends. They've waited for this moment for years. After the prom king and queen have been crowned, John and his three best friends stand at the bar, doing what most high school students do at prom: Drink virgin mojitos. As they swirl their drinks, John makes a sweeping declaration: "Guys, I'm telling you right now: I'm going to be an author!"

"Ha! Yeah right, John! Good luck with that," his friends joke. Everyone laughs, including John, and the moment fades away amidst a night of dancing, reminiscing, and more jokes. The guys have a blast and eventually head their separate ways.

Ten years after graduation, one of John's friends is on a weekend trip to New York City with his family. As they stroll across Times Square, he gasps. Shining down from the massive, seven-story billboard adorning the Nasdaq building is a book cover — with John's name on it.

John's friend can't believe his eyes. As soon as he gets home, he calls his two best buds. "Guys, you will not believe what I just saw. We have to get drinks with John. This is a story we'll want to hear straight from the horse's mouth!"

A few weeks later, the four friends stand at the same bar from prom night all those years ago. After a few inside jokes and old stories, the friend who saw the billboard blurts out: "Alright John, you gotta tell us! How'd you do it man? How did you get your book promoted in Times freakin' Square? I saw it has thousands of ratings already. What is your secret to writing a bestseller?"

John smiles and says: "I only have one rule: Write one page every day."

"Really?" John's friend is baffled. "Like, that's it? I mean, that can't be it, can it?"

"Yup, that's it! I'm afraid there's nothing else to it. Nothing that'd be particularly interesting or useful for me to share, anyway," John says. "But let's not talk about work! I can't believe you married Cathy! Let me get the next round, and then you must tell me how *that* happened. That should be a much more interesting story!" And just like those few seconds all those years ago, when John proclaimed he'd be an author, this moment too passes quickly.

Hours go by, drinks flow (real ones this time), and eventually, everyone is calling it a night. To much cheering and applause, John claims the little reunion is on him, and that he'll pay at the bar after everyone has left.

Right before he does so, the billboard-spotting friend shakes John's hand in private and says: "Congratulations again John, you are so lucky."

Before the second friend leaves, he also shakes John's hand

and remarks: "Congratulations again John, you must have worked incredibly hard for this."

Finally, as the last friend leaves, he walks over to John, shakes his hand, and says: "Congratulations again John. I know you've worked hard for this. You absolutely deserved this opportunity."

The first friend is clever. He knows it takes luck to succeed. Unfortunately, he is *too* clever. His brain tries to shield him from hard work by blinding him to the necessity of effort. Luck is the only thing he sees, and that's why he thinks John is lucky.

The second friend is intelligent. He knows it takes hard work to succeed — but he constantly doubts its veracity. "You *must have* worked hard for this," he said. "But maybe you didn't," he thought in his mind. He is terrified by the sacrifice hard work implies. What if John got divorced over his book? Will hard work ever be worth it? The second friend sees the path, but he does not respect it.

The third friend is wise. He knows it takes both effort *and* luck to succeed. He trusts that, on a long enough timeline, the former will inevitably lead to the latter. He is truly happy for John, and he will continue his own journey as he did before. The third friend both sees the truth and accepts it.

We all have a John in our lives. The question is: Which friend are you?

You Don't Need New Friends

Whenever I catch up with a friend after yet another year has passed, I always make the same joke at the end: "See you next year!" It's funny, sad, and true at the same time.

One time, I messaged an old friend. Instead of agreeing on the usual "We should catch up" that rarely amounts to anything, I hit the call button right then and there, and we ended up chatting for 20 minutes. We talked about our careers, our relationships, and the memories we made together. It was a deep, fun, and invigorating conversation.

After I put down the phone and reflected on our chat, I realized: I have hit the stage in life where I don't need new friends — I need to make sure I don't lose the friends *I have*.

"Our memories are too good to let go," I told my friend on the phone. More important than the memories, however, is the bond we formed because of them. That bond is like a soft pillow in my pocket: Every time I touch it, be it through those memories or an actual catch-up, my heart feels warm and fuzzy. It's inner peace at the push of a button, and in this case, it was the call button of my FaceTime app. That's what we truly care about: The feeling of a unique yet mutual connection.

In high school, we look around, not ahead. We're too busy trying to figure out people in real-time to worry about who might be most valuable down the line. As we grow up and graduate, we get more strategic about our connections. To some extent, this "professionalization" of relationships is normal. But there is also a danger of treating each new person like a door to something else — and forgetting about those you've loved since the early days along the way.

When we wonder why old relationships become harder to maintain and new ones harder to find, we miss a simple truth: We stopped focusing on people and started focusing on ourselves. The older we got, the more forward-looking — and thus self-centered — we became. And then, when we're *actually* old, we wish we hadn't been so forward-looking.

One friend for life is worth a thousand "connections." If you're past high school and college, chances are, you're worrying too much about where you're headed and too little about who you'll leave behind. When we see people only as stepping stones, they'll rightly feel stepped upon, and what good is building bridges if all you'll do is burn them?

You don't need new friends as much as you need to not lose the friends you have. Never put meeting new people over caring for those you already love. Keep your priorities straight. Don't let go of someone you *know* you want in your life at the off chance of adding someone you may or may not like.

Reconnect with the people you love. It's easier than you think. Like our best relationships, the old saying never expires: Make new friends but keep the old, for one is silver while the other is gold.

The 30% Rule

There's a scene in *The Lord of the Rings* where two characters traveling with the hobbits, Gollum and Sméagol, have an argument as the rest of the group sleeps at night.

Gollum tells Sméagol that they should try to steal the "One Ring," the precious good the fellowship carries. To entice him, Gollum reminds Sméagol of what they have done in the past to secure the ring. He calls him a liar and a thief, a murderer even.

"I hate you!" Sméagol retorts. He claims the hobbits are their friends. And then, Gollum whips out the absolute nuke of social interaction: "You don't *have* any friends! Nobody likes *you*!" The twist, of course, is that Gollum and Sméagol are one and the same. The goblin-like creature is talking to itself.

This kind of anti-pep talk is a negativity-breeding exercise most of us are, sadly, somewhat familiar with — and it only gets worse when someone other than our mirror image delivers the blow. If anyone has ever hurled a "Nobody likes you around here!" at your head, whether "around here" was in high school, in college, or at work, you know what I'm talking about: That one really stings.

James Altucher has been the victim of this line many times, and so in his book *Choose Yourself*, he offers a remedy. Actually, his reader Dashama does, a yogi whose daring photos James kept using for his posts, initially without permission. When the two of them started talking, Dashama told James that "we rob ourselves of our joy and happiness when we stop and check in with what everyone else is thinking and saying about us."

Dashama recalled once reading an interview with Gabrielle Reece, a professional volleyball player, model, mother, and wife to a world-class surfer. Asked how she handled the demands of all these roles, Reece said:

"In life, you will always have 30% of people who love you, 30% who hate you, and 30% who couldn't care less."

The idea made a great impact on Dashama. It empowered her to heal from past traumas, regain her physical health with alternative methods, and build a thriving yoga business. Now, whenever someone berates her, she just files it under "the 30% who won't like me no matter what I do or say" and goes about her day.

When he alluded to this "30% rule" on his blog,[1] James said its implications are clear: "You should do what you love. You should do the best you can. And when bad comments come, just put them in the 30% bucket where they belong."

In his book, James further noted that the same dynamic applies not just to you as a person but also to the work you do, especially the creative kind: "No matter who you are, no matter what you do, no matter who your audience is: 30% will love it, 30% will hate it, and 30% won't care." And again, the consequence is obvious: "Stick with the people who love you, and don't spend a single second on the rest. Life will be better that way."

Whether it's Sméagol telling his alter ego to go to hell, Dashama posting photos of herself in sexy yoga poses, or James using whichever picture he thinks will go best with his blog post, they all embody the 30% rule. The next time someone tries to rain on your parade, tell them about it — and if they don't buy it because it leaves 10% of people unaccounted for, remember: In the math of self-esteem, it is perfectly fine to not count everyone's opinion, and, most likely, the voice of criticism is only in your head.

The 4 Monks

Four monks decided to meditate in silence for two weeks. As a symbol of their practice, they lit a candle and began. By nightfall on the first day, the candle flickered and went out.

The first monk said: "Oh, no! The candle is out."

The second monk said: "We're not supposed to talk!"

The third monk said: "Why must you two break the silence?"

The fourth monk said: "Ha! I'm the only one who didn't speak."

The first monk got so distracted by an external event, he was compelled to point it out. Instead, he could have re-lit the candle.

The second monk felt he had to remind everyone of a rule

that had already been broken. Instead, he could have kept meditating.

The third monk was swept away by his anger, which emerged from his mouth like steam forcing its way through a vent. Instead, he could have stayed calm.

The fourth monk got carried away by his ego, which broke out and claimed victory. Instead, he could have enjoyed his success in silence.

They all had different reasons, but each of the four monks shared his thoughts without filtering them, none of which improved the situation. Had there been a fifth, wiser monk, he would have remained silent and kept meditating. In doing so, he would have pointed out the other monks' mistakes without a single word, and without breaking his own quest for better.

The more you talk, the more likely you are to say something stupid. Keep talking long enough, and embarrassing yourself becomes inevitable. Listening, on the other hand, always leads to learning. Wisdom is cultivated in silence. What's more, when you're not talking, you can watch out for the moments when speaking up actually matters. When your words won't just have *any* impact but a significant, positive one.

The less you speak, the smarter you get. And maybe not quite coincidentally, the smarter you get, the less you speak.

Part IV
Reminders

"Whenever you find yourself on the side of the majority, it is time to pause and reflect."

— *Mark Twain*

Don't Forget Your Light Today

In one of the most tragic moments in the Harry Potter series, Harry must feed his headmaster and mentor, Albus Dumbledore, the "Drink of Despair." The evil potion cannot be magically moved or altered in any way. It must be drunk, but the drinker will pay a heavy price. Just shy of killing its consumer, the elixir causes fear, delirium, and extreme thirst, greatly weakening the target.

Naturally, Lord Voldemort has hidden one of his most important belongings in a good bowl of "the Emerald Potion," as it is otherwise known, and while Harry and Dumbledore succeed in sipping the cup, their victory is short-lived. What they hoped to acquire is no longer there, and they now find themselves weak and defenseless, surrounded by, of all things, water.

With an army of Inferi — spellbound corpses — hiding in the dark waters inside the even darker cave, Voldemort has laid the perfect trap, and since Dumbledore is too frail to fight, the inevitable happens: The boy trips, the Inferi grab, and into the depths he goes. Blinking one last time before he's about to drown, Harry spots a flash of red at the surface. Cutting through the darkness above, warmth suddenly fills the water, and a second later, Harry can no longer feel the Inferis' grasp.

When he pokes his head out of the water, Harry can see but one thing: Fire. Burning, raging, darkness-crushing fire. Dumbledore stands in a storm of light. He wields his wand like a lasso, raining wave after wave of scorching inferno upon their opponents. The pair reunite and, together, fend off the attack.

As so often, Harry is a lucky man. Dumbledore brought his light today — and it made all the difference.

―――――

I'm not sure he ever saw the scene, but, given the lyrics to *Nobody Can Save Me*, Linkin Park's late singer Chester Bennington may as well have been in it:

I'm dancing with my demons
I'm hanging off the edge
Storm clouds gather beneath me
Waves break above my head

Opening the album *One More Light*, the band's last record to be released before Bennington died by suicide, the track walks the edge between light and dark. The rhythm is upbeat, the lyrics sad yet hopeful. The song reminds us to bring our sunshine, to conjure our own, protective ring of fire:

I'm holding up a light
Chasing out the darkness inside
And I don't wanna let you down
But only I can save me

Chester struggled with depression all his life. One day, he simply forgot his light. Having listened to him since I was 13, I'm grateful he brought it for so long.

We all have a light. We *are* "One More Light." That's the lesson Dumbledore, and Chester, and so many others teach us time and again. The light is deep inside us, and only we may ignite it.

Been searching somewhere out there
For what's been missing right here

It's a beautiful gift they've left for us. Thank you, Chester. *One More Light.* Don't forget.

We have a candle in our guest bathroom. "Home," it reads. "No matter when and where, it is a safe place. Whatever happened, it is a warm harbor."

Every time I see the flame flickering in the glass, I remember: Home is where the light is — and the light is something we carry. That's the magic of inner radiance: As long as you bring it, there will *always* be light. You can put it in your pocket. Let it do its thing. Just remember to take it with you.

Wherever you go, *let* there be light. Hold it up every day, be it a tiny spark on your shoulder or a wall of fire against the dark.

Don't forget your light today. It might make all the difference.

Life's Worst Trap

Imagine a black-and-white landscape of rolling hills. There is only one tiny spot of color: On a ridge near the horizon, blue skies and green meadows beckon, calling out for you to join them.

That's life — and that's what we mean when we say "the grass is always greener on the other side." No matter where we stand, there's always that little patch of green across the horizon, a faraway destination where the sun always seems to shine.

A better job. The perfect gentleman. A million dollars. The surfing vacation. A new house, better habit, or a few more fans. The Louis Vuitton handbag. The six-pack. The beautiful woman across the street, or a flash of genius that'll solve our most pressing problem.

Whatever its source, we tend to spend our days chasing the light at the end of our tunnel vision. We fight; we struggle; we complain. We throw others under the bus and run them right over, forgetting we're the ones driving it.

We lose ourselves so completely in the pursuit of our goals

that we rarely turn around, and we never stop and just stare, stare at the vast, green beauty all around us and realize that most of the sunshine falls along the way.

One day, we finally arrive. We reach the top of the hill and throw our fists in the air. Blue skies at last! We take a deep breath and enjoy the view, but only for a second. As soon as our eyes wander along the horizon, we realize: "Man, this scene is totally devoid of color! There's only that tiny little speck of green, somewhere in the back…"

Life's worst traps are the ones we assemble right around us. Not the ones we accidentally fall into. Those are bad, sure, but our biggest crime is erecting bars right where we sit. We forge our own cages from desire and ego when we could be making airplanes out of gratitude and presence.

There is, however, one true ray of light at the end of every tunnel: We are free to abandon one for the other at any moment.

Relationships – Trains

Relationships are like trains: You get on, and the ride begins. As long as you stay on board, the train will continue. Indefinitely. It doesn't matter if the other party gets off. You're on the train for as long as you *choose to be*.

I said "party" instead of "person" because we don't form bonds only with people. We have relationships with everything in the universe: Places, jobs, possessions, even habits, memories, and feelings.

If your spouse divorces you, but you think about them every day for the rest of your life and never remarry, did that relationship ever end? I don't think so. You're still on the train. Sometimes, I miss silly little collectibles I owned 25 years ago. Occasionally, I still ride those trains. If running gets you through the stressful demands of college but destroys your knees after you graduate, the habit got off the train. You can stay on it, but running will no longer serve you.

Unlike on a hiking trip, when we know exactly at which stop to get off, it's hard to guess when to leave a relationship. You can do so at any time, but where — or when, rather — is the right station? Is it the one-month mark? The three-year mark? Never?

If you ride a train long enough, at some point, it'll go backwards. Or in a circle. That happens in our relationships too. We repeat the same patterns. We regress. The train will keep going automatically, but it's our job to make sure it keeps going *in the right direction*, and that direction will have to change again and again.

The true danger of relationship trains, however, lies in an attribute they share with real ones: their speed. If you've ever ridden a train into a tunnel, you know what I mean. Everything goes dark from one moment to the next, but you can barely blink a few times before it's over. Suddenly, you're back in the light — and many miles ahead. In that sense, our relationships travel through time, and they drag us right with them.

When it comes to the connections we care about the most, said time tunnels leave us with nostalgia. Your family, partner, kids, and best friend — life always seems to cut these relationships short because, well, they can never last long enough, can they?

Much more problematic, however, are the time tunnels we pass holding on to our unreflected commitments. At the end of those, all we'll find is regret. We often form new relationships thinking, "I'll just move into this flat for now. I'll find a better place soon." "We'll just get dinner and take things from there," we might say, or, "This is just a temporary gig. I'll do this job no longer than a year."

"Just" is the most dangerous word in the English language. In a deliberate life, "just" must be struck from your vocabulary.

Every single one of our relationships matters, yet we often spend little time deciding when, where, and how we begin them — which trains we choose to board. As those trains zip through countless tunnels, those beginnings quickly turn into commitments, and commitments are what life is made of.

Suddenly, years have passed, and we wake up realizing we've lived in the past, hanging around on trains in which we no longer have a place. A dead-end job. A broken marriage. A relationship going nowhere.

We can never pay attention to every tunnel, but we can learn to be more attentive more of the time. Most of all, however, we can be more deliberate in which trains we decide to get on.

Be careful which relationships you board. No matter through how many tunnels they'll carry you, may you find more fond memories than regret at each one's end.

Through Wrong to Right

There's an old Indian saying: "Jab sab galat ho raha ho, tab sab sahi ho raha hai." According to Asha from *Snowpiercer*, it means: "When everything goes wrong, perhaps it's setting itself right."

If you dislocate your shoulder, the medic will warn you before he pops it back in: "This might hurt." A CEO realizing she took the wrong strategic turn may have to fire an entire department. You might feel embarrassed about leaving your job two months in, but maybe someone you met there will hand you the next, much better one.

It doesn't always have to get worse before it'll get better, but when you *feel* it getting worse without knowing where it'll lead, have a little faith: The switches might still be adjusting, but there's a good chance the train will soon be back on track.

The Isms That Ruin Your Judgement

The Free Dictionary counts 3,824 words that end in "-ism."[1] Sexism. Racism. Egoism. Heroism. Realism. Optimism. Altruism. Modernism. Nihilism. Capitalism. The list feels endless.

Behind every ism hides an ideology: A set of rules and guidelines within which you can think and make decisions without ever feeling uncomfortable. In an ideology, each thought goes into a predetermined bucket. The beliefs and attitudes outlining those buckets are time-tested but rigid, leading to black-and-white thinking and a right-or-wrong answer to every question. Therefore, ideologies are very efficient at sorting your thoughts but miserable at determining their accuracy.

Let's say you grew up in a household where your mom lost her job and then started her own business. After long years of hard work and cheap meals, your family can finally afford an upper-middle-class lifestyle. Based on everything you have observed, you now subscribe to individualism — the belief that people should be afforded maximal freedom. That if you are hard-working, self-reliant, and independent, you should get to keep what you achieve.

You can immediately see how this one word, "individualism," will drag behind it a giant rat-tail of consequences in the attitudes-and-beliefs department. You're a self-starter. You don't hesitate to get your hands dirty. You also don't trust people easily and are wary of outside support. The list goes on and on.

This is all well and good, until you meet someone who challenges your ideology. On a slow day at Starbucks, you strike up a conversation with the barista. You learn they escaped from a Third World country because one day, amidst a civil war, a soldier from one of the militias walked into their house and shot their father at point-blank range. What happens then? Well, first, you choke on the speech you were about to give about how, if only they applied themselves more, they could stop being a barista and "amount to something in this world."

Next, the discomfort of the ideology-driven really kicks in: What you gained in inner peace and sometimes real, sometimes fake clarity by subscribing to an ism is now lost as the world confronts you with a new reality. You have merely postponed your struggle, not circumvented it.

Now the question becomes which one do you want more, the truth or the comfort? Will you give up your ism and concede that, actually, this person absolutely hit it out of the park by becoming a Starbucks barista? Or will you brush their truth aside, ignore it, or, worst of all, try to override it with your own by giving your speech regardless?

Ideologies move our discomfort to interactions in the external world because no matter how battle-tested each of their individual rules might be, they all force you to view the world

2-Minute Pep Talks

through only one lens. That's not observation. That is merely poor judgement.

When we don't have ideologies to comfort us, we feel inner unrest all the time. We doubt much of what we know, but we also keep an open mind. We are ready to receive new knowledge as it presents itself and, therefore, more flexible in navigating the world. That too provides comfort, albeit a different kind.

The ism-less only have one option in extracting truth from the world, yet it is, ironically, the most efficient one of them all: trust. You have to trust first in order to find out what's true. This is an involved approach. It requires being responsible, accountable, and even vulnerable. While you can somewhat bolster trust with facts, the only true way to decide when to show faith and when to refuse it is to listen to your gut.

Trust is the opposite of all isms. When life unfolds in front of you, trust doesn't need to ask follow-up questions. Trust requires a leap of faith, a leap you'll only take if you feel that *right now*, you can make it across. No ideology can help you determine if you're ready for that.

That's why the word "trust" does not end in "-ism:" It's a tough teacher, but in the long run, it will always help you see the truth — and your judgement will only improve.

Don't Listen to the Ducks

In one *How I Met Your Mother* episode, the gang around Ted Mosby argues fiercely about which animal is cooler: rabbits or ducks? If you had asked me when I was nine, I would have sided with Marshall, who's defending the lone position that ducks are evil, and rabbits are good.

Back then, we went to a lake on a weekend trip. There were ducks of all shapes, sizes, and colors walking around. I fed some of them, and they flocked towards me. It was a blast. I kept feeding them, and more and more ducks kept coming.

In the blink of an eye, however, the tide turned against me. A big crowd of some 20 ducks backed me into a corner, right against a tree. I stumbled, fell down, and scraped my elbow. Needless to say, I was angry. I hated the ducks. I was crying. The fact that my dad took pictures of the whole thing didn't help much either.

While, like Marshall, I have since come around on ducks the animal, there is a metaphor in this story: Life is full of pushy ducks, but the only one you get to be angry at is yourself.

When you're six, a duck will tell you to put down your imaginary Superman cape because otherwise, you'll never be a big boy. When you're ten, ducks will push you to get a pair of Jordan's because otherwise, you won't be cool. When you're 15, a duck will whisper in your ear to ditch your best friend for the hot guy because otherwise, you're not gonna be prom queen.

When you're 18, all ducks yell only one thing: Get into a good college because otherwise, you'll be a black sheep with a shitty job. When you're 25, a duck will suggest picking the stable gig because otherwise, you'll never be able to start a family. When you're 29, many ducks will chant "Get married fast!" because otherwise, you'll be too old to marry at all.

The list goes on and on. That's what it truly means to have all your ducks in a row: There's always another duck waiting, ready to tell you what to do next. These ducks aren't people, although they sometimes speak through them. They're nothing but ideas, constructs, and ideals, but they can back you into a corner much worse than even the most menacing flock of birds.

What these ducks are pushing you towards is making life's big choices on a whim and then spending the rest of it obsessing over trivialities. If you let them, they will shove you around until you fall over. That's the inevitable consequence when you keep feeding the ducks.

The more things you do because of what you'll be if you don't, the less you'll like who you are when it's too late.

You can check all of society's boxes yet none of your own, and all you'll do is scrape your elbow. Allen Saunders once said that "life is what happens to you while you're busy making other plans." If you're busy making other *people's* plans, you will miss it entirely.

Ultimately, however, life is what remains after our choices

have been made. We can only plan and act so much before the chips fall where they may — but if we don't choose at all, there'll be very little left altogether.

Choose to choose, and even if you think they're cooler than rabbits, don't listen to every duck crossing your path.

4 More Isms

Every word that ends in "-ism" has the potential to become a lifestyle and worldview, a singular Instagram filter through which you'll view your entire life. If it does, that filter will color your every thought and decision. But that's never how it starts.

Ideology begins with a single interaction. Sometimes, it is an interaction of mind and object. Often, it is one between two people. Every spiral needs a starting point, and while a single ism practiced once will not deliver us straight to poor-judgement hell, it can be the trap door opening beneath our feet, sending us onto a slippery slope.

In case of the following four isms, which we have all indulged in and often succumb to on a daily basis, it is far too easy to stay on that slope. To keep sliding until we can no longer get off the chute. This simple, five-sentence story will illustrate what the beginning of the end can look like:

Boy meets girl. They fall in love. Girl can't hold it back any longer.

Criticism
Girl: "I love you."
Boy: "How much?"

Sarcasm
Girl: "I love you."
Boy: "And what's the good news?"

Skepticism
Girl: "I love you."
Boy: "Do you?"

Cynicism
Girl: "I love you."
Boy: "Why would you ever say that?"

The critic believes that good things can happen, but he is never satisfied. Nothing is ever enough. The sarcastic may or may not believe, but he has stopped caring. All that remains is snark.

The skeptic does *not* believe that good things can happen, especially not to him. Even if he can be temporarily convinced, his doubts will haunt him forever. The cynic has stopped believing in anything at all, and so the only thing he can dispense is poison, attacking belief wherever he encounters it.

What's the good ending to this story? We all know what that looks like:

Girl: "I love you."
Boy: "I love you too."

But what does it require? Trust. Trust is proactive. The trusting do not wait to slip up. They are ready to leap whenever the time comes. It's not that the trusting never fall down. It's that they consider getting back up part of the process, even if, sometimes, it means they'll have to crawl back up the slope at a snail's pace.

Yes, with trust as your starting point, you'll often burn your hand, and sometimes traumatically so. Most of the time, however, you'll find reasons to believe, and your belief will be rewarded — because good things not only *can* happen, they *will*.

Life is better without a style, but if you must pick one, please skip all the isms in the dictionary. Make trust your partner in crime, and, ironically, you'll stay out of the prison of misery.

You Can't Outrun Yourself

When I started meditating, one of the first things I realized was this: Your brain is fuller than you could ever imagine. It has been imprinted with trillions of microscopic impressions over decades, and every single one of them is recorded. The mind buries, but it never truly forgets.

The same is true for your body, especially for the experiences heavily processed by both your intellect and your anatomy. "The body keeps the score," Debbie Millman says, quoting the title of a famous book on trauma. On Tim Ferriss's podcast,[1] the pair openly discusses childhood sexual abuse, a tragedy they are, sadly, both familiar with.

"You cannot outrun your own psyche," Debbie continues. "It is just not possible. Your psyche is too strong to just take those experiences and sweep them under a rug and never ever look at them again. They come back."

This is why meditation is one of the easiest habits to practice — you don't need any skills or tools to do it — yet one of the hardest habits to master. Sooner or later, it will send everything you've ever experienced from the depths of your subconscious back to the top of your mind, and there's a lot there that you don't really want to see — which is exactly why you *must*.

Mindfulness is about inner peace more so than about happiness, and the way to achieve inner peace is to remove friction between the mind and everything else, including within the mind itself.

In order to be whole, we must truly allow life to transpire. We cannot be content if we don't process the things that happen to and often *for* us. Good or bad, happy or sad, traumatic or ecstatic, there's a time and place for everything, and, like Mister Rogers said, "anything that's human is mentionable, and anything that is mentionable can be more manageable."

That's also the takeaway from Debbie and Tim's conversation: There is no shame in being human. Trauma comes in a million colors, and even though, thankfully, most of us don't suffer the shades of sexual abuse, we all experience it to varying degrees. We must make space to talk about this particular and any other kind of trauma, and we can be grateful anytime people like Debbie and Tim create an open field for discussion.

You can't outrun yourself, but you can understand that, be it your psyche or your body, allowing it to catch up is a healthy thing.

The Secret of a Happy Life

Logan lived a long, *long* life but never an easy one.

Born an illegitimate child to the groundskeeper of a rich family that ended up taking him in, Logan saw his foster father die before his eyes at 13 years old. Worse, he unknowingly killed his biological father as a result, never truly having gotten to know either.

After fleeing the scene, Logan grew up in a mining colony. He was subject to child labor under gruesome conditions, his only consolation being the company of his best friend. One day his half-brother tracked him down, demanding revenge for their father's killing. In the ensuing altercation, Logan accidentally stabbed his best friend to death.

Logan blamed himself so much, he thought of himself as an animal — a wolverine — more so than a human.[1] He withdrew to the woods and lived alone among wolves. Driven out of hiding, Logan eventually resigned himself to doing the only thing he was good at: fighting. He fought in the Civil War. Then World War I. And World War II. Logan even fought in Vietnam.

Later, Logan was kidnapped, tortured, and experimented

on. Someone turned him into a walking weapon, and he lost his memory because of it.

By the time Logan found his place as part of a force for good in the world, he was over 130 years old. Even from then on, however, most of his life was filled with pain, anger, and sadness. Logan fell in love only to have the woman of his dreams ripped from his life. Once. Twice. The third time it happened, she died by his own hands.

Logan often drowned his sorrows in alcohol, trying to numb the pain and find answers at the bottom of a bottle. He rarely discovered any, however, and when he did, they only led to more questions.

Logans life was one giant, lonely battle. A physical battle. A battle with the bottle. A battle against the odds, against himself, and against hopelessness. Fighting. More fighting. Every day he fought.

Looking at a life like Logan's, it really makes you wonder: Where did he find the will to continue? Why keep fighting? Because that's what he did. Despite everything, Logan never stopped fighting, and I think I know why.

For all the pain he endured, for all the tragedy and suffering, there was one thing never absent from Logan's life: meaning. No matter how hard his struggle, Logan always had a reason to fight. To go on. Someone worth protecting. Someone — or something — worth fighting *for*.

Even on the day he died, Logan was still fighting. Right after a fight for his family, he finally uttered his last words: "Don't be what they made you."

Logan never asked for his life to be full of hardships. Who would? He didn't *want* all the trouble. All the grief, rage, and despair. Logan was a good man to whom many bad things happened, but he never let that stop him. Not once.

The world put tremendous pressure on Logan, trying to crush him underneath its weight. But he never turned into what the external forces seemed to want him to be. He never became what the world wanted to make him. Regardless of how many labels and heavy burdens it heaped upon him, Logan kept going. That's why we tell stories about people like him long after they're gone.

The secret of a happy life is that it might not be happy at all. But even if the road is long, arduous, and full of twists we do not understand, it may still be a road worth traveling in the end. We'll never know until we get there, but the only way to find out is to keep going.

Don't be what they made you. Happiness is not guaranteed, but meaning is available to all.

Are You Free to Abstain?

The French scientist Pierre Fouquet was an early researcher of alcoholism in the 1950s. Fouquet broke the illness into three categories, two of which described the circumstances of people we might call "alcoholics" today. An example would be someone drinking hard liquor in secret with the goal of either forgetting or blacking out, later accompanied by feelings of guilt and shame.

The third category, "alcoholitis," Fouquet described as "the most common form of alcoholism in France, particularly among men." Characteristics of alcoholitis are a high tolerance for alcoholic drinks and a lack of serious psychological complications. Those affected mainly consume beer and wine in social settings, just in too large quantities for their drinking to still be considered "healthy."

What's remarkable about alcoholitis, Fouquet remarked, is the strength of its ripple effect: "We drink to drink with others, but the toxic effects of consumption are still felt." This sums up our sneakiest addictions: We use a behavior to achieve some secondary outcome, and before we know it, what started as a lever has become a pattern from which we can no longer easily extricate ourselves, and the effects of which "are still felt."

If you drink with coworkers four nights a week and have two beers each time, that might seem like a perfectly normal thing to do, and yet it will affect your sleep, productivity, and mood. Do this a few weeks in a row, and you'll still be far from considering your alcohol consumption a problem, but deep down, the after-work beers will feel less and less optional.

The question — and this may be Fouquet's greatest contribution to the world — is this: Do you have the freedom to abstain?

It is the loss of this freedom that marks our departure from normalcy and descent into addiction, he claimed. When we no longer feel free to abstain, when it seems as if there is no choice to be had, that's when we should scratch our heads — because we *always* have a choice.

A friend of mine loves both a good wine and a nice pack of gummy bears, but every year on January 1st, he swears off both for 100 days. I love coffee. I usually drink two cups a day. Every now and then, however, I'll skip a day or even a week. Not because I want to quit coffee, but because I must remember that I *can*.

It's important to give yourself a break, even from the things you love. Letting go, if only temporarily, will prevent those things from becoming chains around your ankles. Nothing is more liberating than to sit in front of a foregone conclusion, like "I will drink this beer," and realize that "You know what? I'm free to abstain. I can just say no."

Don't let harmless habits become disastrous dictators. Use your freedom to abstain. Even when the drink feels like destiny, it is something you'll always have — no matter how long ago you think you might have lost it.

Your Phone Should Be Like Your Toothbrush

If your phone was more like your toothbrush, your life would be a lot better. Your toothbrush is the greatest tool of all time. You only use it when you're *supposed to* for as long as you *need to*, and then you let it go.

This is what outstanding tools do: They put you in control at all times, even the times when you're not using them which, nowadays, is actually half the battle. When attention is our scarcest resource, the best tools must optimize for mindfulness. They need to protect our time, awareness, and energy instead of draining them.

Your toothbrush does this via the three properties of great tools: It only alerts you when you would benefit from using it, it takes as little of your time and energy as possible during usage, and, finally, it prompts you to put it down once you're done.

Sitting on your bathroom sink, your toothbrush only "calls" to you twice a day: Once when you get ready in the morning, and once again at night. If it's electric, it might have a 2-minute timer, and if not, you'll naturally feel when you've brushed every tooth. Finally, since there's nothing else you can do with a toothbrush, you'll set it down automatically when you're ready.

Your phone, on the other hand, does the opposite of all these things, at least in its standard configuration. It calls for your attention all the time with sounds and notifications, and once it has you in its grip, it never wants to let you go. Often, you'll "wake up" after ten minutes of mindless browsing, only to realize you've forgotten why you picked it up in the first place.

We now spend between three and six hours on our phones, *every single day*.[1] That's some 30 hours per week, which means on top of your normal job, you basically work full-time at a call center. That is insane. Luckily, there is a way to bring the properties of great tools to your smartphone, and it only takes a few taps:

1. **Disable (almost) all notifications**. The only time your phone should tell you, "Hey, come check me!" is when it matters. That means for calls, meetings, and anything time-sensitive, which 99% of things aren't.
2. **Eliminate vibration entirely**. Phones now vibrate so strongly, they might as well ring. Turn it off. Demand actual silence. Force yourself to make a deliberate decision every time you pick up your phone.
3. **Hide your phone from view for most of the day**. Out of sight, out of mind. It really is that simple. Put it in your bag, hide it behind your laptop, or keep it in another room. If it's not there, you won't miss it.

No matter what you are doing in life, you don't need a permanent, audiovisual cue vying for your attention. You need that attention, and you need *all of it*.

Think. Focus. Engage. These are the true tasks of the mind.

When we discovered fire, we found ourselves with more power in our hands than we could handle. Smartphones, however, are something we invented. They're not a force of nature but a tool to be configured and wielded well. When we put them in toothbrush mode, all we're doing is show them their rightful place. Let's do so before we get burned.

When the Phone Rings

What's your first thought when the phone rings? If it is "Something's wrong" or, worse, "What did *I* do wrong?" you are not alone. Our minds are programmed to treat even the tiniest of stressors as potential death threats. In a split second, they race from "I screwed up" to "I'll be fired" to "I will be homeless" to "I'm going to die."

While our survival instinct got us into the 21st century, this instant-anxiety-button is now ruining our lives instead of saving them. When we simulate only the worst possible futures before deciding whether to fight or take flight, struggling and running begin to feel like our only options — and in both scenarios, stress and adrenaline will soar.

Like any good obstacle, however, our neanderthal brain also holds the solution to the very predicament it creates. In his book *What Every Body Is Saying*, ex-FBI agent and body language expert Joe Navarro explains what happens right in the split second before we spiral into anxiety: We freeze.

> *"One purpose of the freeze response is to avoid detection by dangerous predators or in dangerous situations. A second purpose is to give the threatened individual the opportunity to assess the situation and determine the best course of action to take."*

Opportunity. Assess. Determine. That sounds more like the kind of brain we need in our civilized environment, don't you think? To leverage the opportunity the freeze response provides, we must use its brief presence to shift our attention away from "fight-or-flight" and towards what Stanford psychologist Kelly McGonigal calls "the pause-and-plan response" in her book *The Willpower Instinct*. Think of it as a better gut reaction for the modern world.

The pause-and-plan response allows you to perceive what's really going on — "an internal conflict, not an external threat." McGonigal says the best way to trigger the pause-and-plan response is to do what you always do: breathe.

When a piercing ringtone breaks the silence, our breath goes flat. We inhale shallowly yet hectically, but it only takes a single gulp of air to break the pattern. When we breathe deeply and slowly, we "activate the prefrontal cortex and increase heart rate variability, which helps shift the brain and body from a state of stress to self-control mode." McGonigal suggests that after about two minutes of doing so, we'll "feel calm, in control, and capable of handling cravings or challenges."

The big takeaway here is that if you catch it at the onset, you can actually parlay your anxiety into making better decisions. What a plot twist! And all you have to do is pause.

Seth Godin once put it like this:[1] "All anxiety is is experiencing failure in advance." That's what the extra breaths are for. To briefly feel the failure long before you've failed. To let the anxiety wash over you so it may also wash away. That's modern-world survival.

Catch your freeze response, then shift your attention inward. Give yourself the gift of "more flexible, thoughtful action." Inhale slowly, and remember: Every choice you make will feel better after a single, deep breath.

Shibuya

Every day, over a million people cross the intersection outside Shibuya Station in Tokyo. With up to 3,000 people passing over in a single cycle, it is the busiest pedestrian crossing in the world.

Whenever the light turns green, a little race begins. Who will get across the quickest? Who will take the straightest line? Who will manage to wiggle through the crowds untouched, and who will bump into a stranger?

Nowhere does the race have more participants than in Shibuya, but every day, the same contest happens billions of times around the globe. The race takes place at intersections in Mexico City, in rural Canada, and in Cape Town. It happens in Hawaii, Paris, and even your town, no matter how small it might be.

The next time you get a chance, observe the different players. Who just stares into space before the light turns green? Who is completely absorbed in their phone? Who is lost in thought or conversation, and who can't wait to continue their morning run? Almost without fail, you'll notice one thing:

The person who first makes it to the other side is someone who paid attention.

Try to be that person. Not to win. Not because you'll be halfway across by the time other players look up. Do it because paying attention is the single-best way to improve your thinking.

There are many ways to increase your brain power. You can train your memory, practice deliberately, tackle big goals, think positively, eat light, meditate — the list goes on and on. But all of these tactics pale in comparison to relentlessly using your best asset: your attention.

If you truly want to do a service to yourself, others, and your mind, fully dedicate it to the task at hand — even if it's just waiting for the traffic light to change.

Be Water, My Friend

Water is balance. That's why Bruce Lee's "Be Water" analogy is popular to this day. His metaphor perfectly captures the balance we all need in our lives.

Water doesn't look left or right. It just makes its way however it can. It adapts, but it always perseveres. Even at rest, water still slowly eats away at its surroundings. In *Striking Thoughts*, a collection of Lee's notes and writings, he expanded on the short recorded clip:[1]

> *"Be like water making its way through cracks. Do not be assertive, but adjust to the object, and you shall find a way around or through it. If nothing within you stays rigid, outward things will disclose themselves."*

Water is a slow judge. It feels out its obstacle, one drop at a time. Then, it wraps itself around it, if only to later crush the barrier. Essentially, water asks: "What shape do I need to be?" That's a question you can only ask, however, if you come to each situation with an empty mind.

> *"Empty your mind. Be formless. Shapeless. Like water. You put water into a cup, it becomes the cup. You put water into a bottle, it becomes the bottle. You put it in a teapot, it becomes the teapot. Water can flow, or it can crash."*

Despite having no form of its own and being infinitely soft, water is one of, if not *the* strongest element on earth. It can trickle, it can flow, and it can rage. If water drops on a stone long enough, it'll hollow it out. If water forms a wave the size of a building, it can crush an entire ship. Water is indifferent to form. It becomes whatever it needs to be to keep moving forward.

> *"Water may seem to move in contradiction, even uphill, but it chooses any way open to it so that it may reach the sea. It may flow swiftly or it may flow slowly, but its purpose is inexorable, its destiny sure. Be water, my friend."*

Thanks to its never-ending balancing act, water always finds its way home. Sooner or later, it *will* reach the sea. You too should keep flowing. Have plans, but don't force them.

Life is unpredictable. Sometimes it throws stones in your way, and sometimes it opens a new door for you. When you're water, you're ready for either one of the two. Whatever happens tomorrow, you'll adapt.

When the universe says "Yes," go. Flow downhill. Move fast. Leap. Ride the momentum, take the opportunity, and make the most of your advantage.

When the universe says "No," listen. Take a different path. Adjust. Persist slowly instead of failing spectacularly.

When a crisis hits, summon your strength. Form a towering

wave. And when the sea is calm, enjoy the cruise and take in the view.

When you're water, you're always exactly where you're meant to be.

Be water, my friend.

Part V
Hope

"It's amazing how a little tomorrow can make up for a whole lot of yesterday."

— John Guare

How To Not Waste Your Life

If you've wasted your whole life, can you make up for it in a single moment? This is the question at the heart of *Extraction*, a Netflix blockbuster which, at nearly 100 million viewers in the first month, marked the company's biggest film premiere ever at the time it was released.[1]

Following Chris Hemsworth as a black-market mercenary trying to rescue the kidnapped son of India's biggest drug lord, the movie is full of car chases, gun fights, and a whopping 183 bodies dropping at the hands of Thor himself. At the end of the day, however, it is *about* none of those things. It's a movie about redemption.

After freeing his target, the 15-year-old Ovi, from the hands of a rival Bangladeshi drug baron, Hemsworth's character Tyler shows true vulnerability in a brief moment of shelter. When Ovi asks him if he's always been brave, Tyler claims he's "just the opposite," having left his wife and six-year-old son — right before the latter died of lymphoma.

Sharing the kind of wisdom only children tend to possess, Ovi replies with a Paulo Coelho quote he's read in school:

> "You drown not by falling into the river, but by staying submerged in it."

You're not an ex-Special Forces agent. Your life is not a movie. There will be no obvious signs. No excessive violence. No rampant drug abuse. Just a slow, steady trickle of days, each a little more like the last, each another step away from your dreams — another day submerged in the river.

The river is pressing "Ignore" on the reminder to decline a good-but-not-great project request. The river is saying, "When I've done X, I'll start writing." The river is postponing asking your daughter about her dance hobby because today, you're just too tired.

The river is everything that sounds like a temporary excuse today but won't go away tomorrow. Trust me. I've been there. It really, *really* won't. No matter how much you'd like it to.

At first, it won't feel like you're drifting. You're just letting go for a bit. You're floating. The river carries you. It's nice. Comfortable. Things happen. Time passes. It'll keep passing.

Eventually, however, the river will lead into a bigger river. Now you're in new terrain. You've never seen this place before. Where can you get ashore? Where will this river lead?

Soon, you'll no longer be able to see what's next. The waters get wild and foggy. You have no idea what's coming. The river could widen, deepen, bend, twist, or dry up. It could turn into a waterfall and send you right off a cliff, never to return. You might stay submerged forever.

All rivers flow into the sea. If you don't push against its current, if you don't swim towards the surface, that's where you're going.

There won't be a big shootout at the end. Just a regretful look out the window. A relative visiting. "Oh yeah, *that*. I never did it. I can't tell you why."

No one is coming to save you. You won't get an extraction. No one will beat you into writing your book or asking her to marry you or being a good mother. No 15-year-old boy will serve you the answer via a quote from a book.

The only way to not waste your life is to not waste today. Write a sentence. Make a hard choice. Pick up the phone.

We all fall into the river from time to time. But we can't stay submerged in it. Don't let small regrets pile up in silence. Take one step each day. One stroke towards the surface.

You're not a soldier, and no single brief can save you. No standalone mission will define your legacy.

Don't hope for a shot at redemption. Redeem yourself with your actions. Redeem yourself every day.

If You Can't Beat the Fear, Just Do It Scared

Glennon Doyle knows fear all too well. The fear of eating, the fear of drinking, and the fear of speaking. The fear of saying what she wants, the fear of changing her mind, and the fear of admitting her marriage isn't working.

Doyle struggled with bulimia, alcoholism, and other addictions. Her ex-husband was unfaithful. How would they continue to raise their three daughters? How could she explain she now loved a woman? More so than most people, Doyle needed her own advice: "If you can't beat the fear, just do it scared."

I don't know if your fears will be less traumatic than hers, but I do know this: Today, fear rarely tell us what's dangerous — it tells us what's important. If you follow the fear, you'll find the growth. In fact, it's one of few compasses reliably pointing in the right direction.

The scariest thing for a blogger is to write a novel. The scariest thing for a developer is to quit her job in hopes of better. A month-long solo trip for a busy stay-at-home dad?

Blasphemy! And yet, they might all be steps towards our true north.

When you feel the fear, can you lean forward? Or at least not run away? It's the better of our usual two options: to escape or wait until the dread fades. While you're waiting, however, consider that the fear might not dissolve. Why won't it subside? Well, how could it? It's here to show you the way.

Whenever you're ready, fear will lend you a hand. Oh, it's coming along. You bet. Ain't no solo seats on this ride. Once you accept that part, you can let fear do its job. Let it be your guide instead of your game over. Don't just tolerate the skepticism. Welcome it! Cherish it. Use doubt to keep your head on straight, and always keep growing towards the scary bright light.

Someone Will Save You Today

If his mom hadn't called him about the suicide book he'd ordered from the library, Tim Ferriss might not be here today. Thankfully, most of us will never need such a chance encounter or staged intervention. But why? Why don't we all require literal life-saving, given we all fight the same existential battles?

I have a theory: You're *already* being saved. It just happens differently than you imagine, and you don't realize it does. Every day, tiny parachutes protect you from falling. You don't know who made them. You don't see them on your back. All you know is you're okay, and that's the part that matters.

When I was 13, I felt angry. I don't know why or at who. Every morning, I listened to Linkin Park. For some reason, it felt soothing to hear another man yell at the top of his lungs. Then, one day, my anger just...went away. Did Linkin Park save me? I think it did. Not in a dramatic, literal way, but with countless tiny parachutes — one song, one scream, one minute at a time.

At this very second, something is saving you too. Maybe it's a song. Maybe it's a joke. It might be a friend listening to your troubles. We can rarely see it, but all through our lives, a stream of invisible, helping hands carries us. Like Tinkerbell adding a dash of stardust to every one of Peter Pan's steps, they sprinkle microscopic sparks of salvation across our days, and it is thanks to these sparks that we don't need a more radical and tragic kind of saving.

Art is salvation. Kindness is salvation. So are joy, laughter, and motion. Whoever bestows them upon us is our savior; whoever makes us laugh, smile, or calm down becomes a helping hand. Of course, we too are a hand lifting others. We're all doing our part, even if we don't realize it.

It's a magnificent contradiction: When it comes to the big things in life, no one will come and save you. You must be your own light. No one will make you rich, happy, healthy, or fulfilled. Those torches only you can carry. At the same time, you are *constantly* being saved. Every day, billions of humans send trillions of ripples across the universe. Some of them will always reach you. Some of them will carry you forward.

Saving is for all of us, and yet saving, like everything, is part of the great balance. Every day, we're both the savior and the saved. By the time you rest your head on your pillow tonight, you will have been saved. You'll also have saved someone else. Neither of you will know who did it. Neither will have seen the other pull it off.

All you'll know is you're okay — and that's the part that matters.

One More Time

You pushed yourself up. One step. Two. Then, you fell. You didn't know what compassion was, and that made it easy: You just got back up. That day, you forgave yourself — for the very first time.

You took all the candy. "Did you eat the gummy bears?" You shook your head no. Oh, that damned first lie. Of course your parents knew. They let it go, but you didn't. Couldn't. Until, eventually, you forgave yourself — one more time.

You said you'd be home by ten, but you weren't. They were worried sick. When you arrived, you took your scolding and went to bed. Your stomach twisted into a knot. That hurt way more than being grounded. A few days later, you forgave yourself — one more time.

On your third date, he told you he was seeing someone else. How could he do that to you? What did you do wrong? For weeks, you turned over every option in your head. One day, you realized the answer was "Nothing." So you forgave yourself — one more time.

The girl you liked was never into you. You just refused to

hear the message. When it finally sank in, you broke down and cried. All this time, wasted. But finally, you knew. And you forgave yourself — one more time.

You felt lonely and isolated. Why didn't anyone understand? Eventually, it dawned on you: You never told them. Instead, you pushed them away. But time heals all wounds, even if not all bridges can be rebuilt. So you found a new start, a new chapter, a new life...and forgave yourself — one more time.

You knew you weren't fit to work, but you showed up anyway. You wanted to look professional and strong. The project went sideways — obviously. You blew past the deadline. The final number was wrong. Your boss ripped your head off. Worse, she was right. But you could still do better next time. Take the day when you're sick. You vowed not to repeat the same mistake. Then, you forgave yourself — one more time.

The voice in your head said no. That you couldn't do it. "Who should believe you? Why would anyone care?" It brought up some nasty things, and you surrendered. To the couch. To Netflix. To ice cream. Yet, when the sun rose the next morning, you were still here. You had a chance to try again. But in order to take it, you had to forgive yourself — one more time.

You should be so much further by now. More money. A family. The job you really wanted. You don't have any of these things, and yet, life is still beautiful. There's so much more to it than this. What if the signs don't point to regret? Maybe, the pressure is all in your head. The clock always strikes forgiveness — one more time.

You're not alone in this, you know? Whatever "this" is, right now, someone out there feels the same. But if you don't raise your hand, they can't see you. Can't help you. Can't tell you they're going through a similar thing. Don't stay quiet. You don't have to be ashamed. Speak up. Trust in forgiveness. And if they mock you? Then you can still forgive yourself — one more time.

Whatever happens today, or tomorrow, or 36 days from now, please promise me one thing: Promise me, you'll forgive yourself — one more time.

If You're Not Valued, You're in the Wrong Place

When she graduated high school, the father told his daughter: "I'm proud of you. Soon, you will move out and go your own way. I'd like to give you a going-away present. Follow me."

The father walked to the garage and pressed a light switch the daughter had never seen before. A single light bulb lit up and revealed: Hidden in the back of the garage, there sat an old car. It was dusty, dirty, and clearly not in good shape.

Dangling a set of keys in his hand, the father smiled: "I bought this car many years ago. It is old, but now it's yours! I only have one request: Take it to the used car lot and ask how much they're willing to give you for it. I'd like to know."

The daughter was happy to finally have her own car, but she wished it was a better one. With a sigh and an awkward half-smile, she took the keys and drove downtown. When she returned, she said: "They offered me $1,000, dad. They said it looks pretty rough."

"Hmm, okay," her father said. "Might you take it to the pawnshop instead? Just to hear what they have to say." The daughter rolled her eyes and went off. When she came back, she said: "The pawnshop was even worse. They only wanted to pay $100 because the car is so old."

"Okay then," the father said, "only one last try: Please take old Nelly down to the car club, and show her to the members there." "Old Nelly? Really, dad?" At this stage, the daughter genuinely didn't see the point anymore, but because the car was a gift, she did as her father asked.

When she returned, the father could see the surprise on her face. "Well?" "Dad! You won't believe this! Five people in that club offered me $100,000 on the spot! They said it's a Nissan Skyline GTR, and every collector worth their salt would give an arm and a leg for such a rare, iconic car."

The father merely smiled, waited for a moment, and said: "If you are not being valued, you're just in the wrong place. Do not be angry. Do not be bitter. But do go to another place."

"The right place with the right people will always treat you the way you deserve. Know your worth, and never settle where you're not appreciated. Never stay where people don't value you."

The daughter never sold the car, and she never forgot this lesson.

Change Is Resistance

Our lives aren't written in stone. Eventually, we've just lived so long that it feels like they are. But a 90-year-old can pick up the trumpet. A 50-year-old can start a company, and a 20-year-old can advise one.

It's never too late to try something new. Don't let anyone tell you otherwise. Not your friends. Not your parents. Especially not "society," whoever that is. Don't even trust your own mind.

There are no rules. Resist. You can do *anything*. Don't forget.

The Meaning of Life

Why get out of bed if you don't have to?
Why have a different breakfast than yesterday?
Why go to work when you could be fired?
Why take the train if you have a car?
Why say hello to someone you see every day?
Why stay late when your salary is fixed?
Why try sushi if you might not like it?
Why ask her out when she'll likely say no?
Why read a book when you have a TV?
Why plan a vacation when it might not happen?
Why go out when it rains?
Why ask the doctor for his opinion?
Why write a diary if no one will read it?
Why celebrate when it's just another day?
Why buy a new notebook when your old one's not full?
Why finish today if you can do it tomorrow?
Why take a plane when it could crash?
Why make a video no one might watch?

Why call when he may not pick up?
Why try a new recipe when you know what she likes?
Why cook if you can just order?
Why write an op-ed when no one asked for your opinion?
Why work out when your tracker is broken?
Why play board games when your kids soon move out?
Why do it now when your idea is four months old?
Why sing if no one can hear it?
Why dance if no one will see?
Why kiss your wife when you'll still be married tomorrow?
Why smile when wearing a mask?
Why think when each thought is fleeting?
Why laugh when no one gets the joke?
Why repair a car that keeps breaking?
Why protest if you're the only one with objections?
Why make a sign nobody may read?
Why hold her hand if she'll forget your name?
Why send a letter that may get lost in the mail?
Why catch a fish if you're planning to release it?
Why compete when you're unlikely to win?
Why help a customer after hours?
Why pay extra to change the color?
Why make a deal with nothing to gain?
Why keep the shares when they're losing money?
Why hold on to old photographs?
Why remember what's not on the test?
Why do it if your boss said no?
Why hit send when you're afraid of the response?
Why propose an idea they might laugh at?
Why quit a safe job to start your own business?
Why suggest a law most people won't like?

Why give a speech when no one might listen?
Why plant a tree whose shade you won't sit in?

Because life is about taking chances.

Your Best Thought

What's your best thought today? You should write it down. Maybe not for the world but definitely for yourself. One thought. One thought can change everything.

Scribble your thought on a scrap of paper. Put it in a jar. Wait for 30 days, 60 days, even 365 days, then take it out again. Look at it. Remember. Ask questions.

Is it still a good thought? Is it worth thinking again? Has it served its purpose? Did it help you through a bad day? Was it one of your best insights? Or maybe one of your worst? Did the thought accompany you all this time? Has it stuck with you? Or does it feel like a distant dream?

Your thought can be simple. "I'm okay." "Coffee is delicious." "Don't argue when you're hungry." Your thought can also be deep. "I hate cycling because I fell off my bike when I was nine." "I'm still in love with him." "I'm more afraid of success than failure." Sometimes, your thought will be an idea. "Coffee should taste like chocolate." "Can I use my phone to make a TV show?" "What if umbrellas were less clunky?" One thought. One thought can change everything.

How many thoughts do you have each day? 6,000?[1] 12,000? 50,000? No one really knows, but it sure is a lot of them.[2] What is your best one today? Think! You only need one thought to mold your future more deliberately.

Write down your thought. Record it. Type it. Pin it. You might not remember it tomorrow. In fact, you may never look at it again. Your thought won't make a big difference next week, maybe not even six months from now — but eventually, it will.

One day, you'll look back through your pile of one-liners. You'll stand under a waterfall of thoughts. Some memories will hit hard. Some ideas will feel refreshing. Old beliefs will roll off your shoulders. "Oh, so that's where my attitude came from. That's why I did this thing." You'll think. Reflect. Act. You'll be a curator of your curated thoughts, and, finally, you'll understand: One thought. One thought can change everything.

If you want to change not just yourself but the world, you should share your one thought. Don't do it for your ego. Do it for us. Help us change, too. It works better when we exchange our thoughts.

Take your time. Work up the courage. At first, no one will see your daily thought. Then, a few people may find it. Then, a few more. Eventually, you might attract a loyal audience. They may even line up for your thoughts.

Maybe someone in that line will have the same thought. What if they go back to their jar, pull out a note, and read the same sentence? Suddenly, you'll be connected. Two humans, one thought. One thought can change everything.

You can write your thought into your diary. You can post it on Twitter. You can turn your thought into an article or let it collect digital dust on your hard drive. Whatever you do, keep collecting your thoughts.

One day, you'll wake up, and life will never be the same. It won't have felt like it back when you started, but now you'll know for sure: It only takes a single one. One thought. One thought can change everything.

Now Would Be a Great Time to Give Up

11:29 on a Thursday. PM, of course. You don't feel like writing. You really, *really* don't. You look terrible too. Desperate. Exhausted. Who even sits at their desk this late on a Thursday, typing against the clock on an orange-lit screen? You do, apparently.

You're tired, but you can't close the laptop. You feel spent but not done. You're wondering not just what to produce but whether you can even produce *something* — and if you could, would it be any good?

Now would be a great time to give up. To close the laptop, go to bed, and get some rest. But what if you don't?

11:46. Tick-tock. Tick-tock. Nobody is forcing you to write. You don't *need to*, especially not right now. The world will keep spinning either way. No one will even notice if you stop. Your parents won't lecture you. Your boss won't berate you. Your readers won't bang down your door. It's just you — but you'll always know.

The problem with the world is that it was spinning before

you were born, and it will still be spinning long after you die. That makes it such a great, universal excuse, and therefore kind of none at all.

It's not like someone glued the pen to your hand the first time. You never had to write. You chose to. You chose to *despite* the world spinning, not because of it. Just like, right now, you're sitting there *despite* your poor condition. You don't even know who you're spiting. Is it the world? Yourself? Your first-grade teacher? All you know is your spite has added up to more good than bad. Do you need another reason?

11:55. Now would be a great time to give up. But what if you don't? What if you sit here, just a little longer? What if some words magically fall onto the page? What if, what if, what if.

Why is there no alternate timeline you can track yourself against? No lifetime tree of your decisions, each fork labeled "gave up" or "didn't give up?" Maybe because deep down, you know you don't need it. You're already convinced: The version of yourself that gave up each time would be in a much darker place than you are now. Tired but typing. 12:05 AM.

Haven't you earned the right to quit? Perhaps — but you've also earned the chance to do one more thing. Today, you chose to take that chance. Scoreboard +1. It's a great mystery, all this. How will the +1s add up? Definitely not like your first-grade teacher explained. Sometimes, one plus one equals zero, and sometimes, three ones will warp you to 54. Maybe that's why the questions linger: Because the good what-ifs outweigh the bad.

12:19. This is it. You've got an idea. You don't care how you look. You no longer worry about what people think. Let the world spin forwards, backwards, or turn upside down. It doesn't matter. You don't know who's going through what *you're* going through, but you know there were many others before you, and they all had to write one more time.

12:24. Now would be a great time to give up. But what if you don't?

Tomorrow Can Be a Good Day

Even long before I started writing, I've always held this one belief. I've known it for as long as I can remember, and I don't have any other lens to view life through. It's as simple as it is powerful, and I can describe it in one sentence: Tomorrow can be a good day.

When I was six, I fell off my bike and tore my chin. We had to wait at the ER for hours. A guy was wheeled in on a stretcher. Motorcycle accident. I don't know if he made it. But as I was licking on my ice cream, I wholeheartedly believed that — both for him and I — tomorrow could be a good day.

When I was 13, a girl broke my heart. Then again at 14. And at 15. And at 16. Sometimes, I thought I'd die alone. I cried over it. But I always believed that, no matter how sad the music I was playing, tomorrow could be a good day.

When I was 26, I lost faith in myself. I wasn't sure if I could go on working so much. I was burned out, desperate, and no longer saw the point. But I still believed that, even if it all went to hell, tomorrow could be a good day.

I know these are laughable stories. They're nothing against

rape, war, rehab, abuse, or depression. I don't know what those feel like. I can only imagine, and I know imagination doesn't quite cut it. But I think *daring* to imagine *without* having lived through it is exactly where my strength lies. If being free of life's heaviest burdens allows me to spread hope, positivity, and optimism, then that's what I'm gonna do. The *only* thing I will do. The reason I was put on this earth.

Tomorrow can be a good day. If I had to erase everything I've ever written except one thing — my epitaph, if you will — this would be it. I believe in it so much, even typing it makes me tear up a little. I can't tell you how desperately I want you to believe it too. I wish I could hold your hands when you feel at your worst, look you in the eye, and say it: "Tomorrow can be a good day."

I can't tell you how or why it works. I can't tell you where I got it from. I just know that, as long as you want me to, I will be here, repeating it for you. Again and again and again. Tomorrow can be a good day.

When your boyfriend breaks up with you, I'll tell you that tomorrow can be a good day. When your doctor says you need surgery, I'll tell you that tomorrow can be a good day. When your boss fires you, your landlord kicks you out, and your dad won't lend you 50 bucks, I will be here and tell you: Tomorrow can be a good day.

Please keep going. Just a little. One more day. One more night. One more time. Sunshine is coming. No matter how dark it feels right now, the light is not far away. It might be right around the corner. Keep walking. Talking. Take one step at a time. One step is enough for today. And tomorrow? Tomorrow can be a good day.

Pep Talk

You can smile.
You can laugh.
You can dance.
You have the capacity to be happy.

You aren't normal, but you're also not weird.
You're human. That's the only thing there is.
You look like you. Not good or bad. Not pretty or ugly. Just you.
You smell like you.
You talk like you.
You move like you.
You do you. Don't forget.

You're allowed to fail.
You're allowed to hurt.
You're allowed to have flaws.
You can change.
You can let go.
You can hit pause.

You can quit.
You can start over.
You can choose something different than you did yesterday.
You control more than you think you do — and everything you don't doesn't matter.

You mean something to someone.
Someone looks up to you.
Someone wants to be more like you.
Someone is betting on you.
Someone believes in you.
Someone wants to help you.
Someone wants to see you succeed.
Someone longs for you.
Someone misses you.
Someone accepts you.
Someone loves you.
Someone will cry when you die.

You're allowed to cry.
You're allowed to love.
You're allowed to miss people when they're gone.
You're not alone.
You can share your weight.
You're not the only one.

You can connect.
You can speak up.
You can lend a helping hand.
You can forgive.
You can forget.
You can try again.

You can change others.
You can lead.
You can be a good example. It's never too late for that, you know?

You have something to share.
Your input matters.
You make a difference. You always have and always will.

You can love.
You can heal.
You can persist.
You are loved.
You are here.
You are missed.

You are the one we need.

I just wanted you to know.

What's Next?

Thank you for reading this book. If you liked *2-Minute Pep Talks*, you might also enjoy my daily blog. You can find it at: **nik.art**

If you want to get updates on new books, you can be my email friend. Join over 25,000 fellow subscribers at: **nik.art/friends/**

About the Author

Niklas Göke writes for dreamers, doers, and unbroken optimists. His work has been featured on Medium, Quora, and CNBC and has attracted thousands of loyal readers. He also runs Four Minute Books, a website with over 1,000 free summaries of the world's best books, each of which you can read in 4 minutes or less to learn 3 valuable lessons.

Web: nik.art
Books: amazon.com/author/nik
Goodreads: goodreads.com/niksblog

Footnotes

Introduction

1. Nain, P. (2022, March 24). Bring in the pep talk. Better Humans. https://betterhumans.pub/bring-in-the-pep-talk-646560c8dbfb
2. Lally, P., van Jaarsveld, C. H. M., Potts, H. W. W., & Wardle, J. (2010). How are habits formed: Modelling habit formation in the real world. European Journal of Social Psychology, 40(6), 998—1009. https://doi.org/10.1002/ejsp.674

A Word About Pep Talks

1. McGinn, D. (2017, July 1). The science of pep talks. Harvard Business Review. https://hbr.org/2017/07/the-science-of-pep-talks

Mister Rogers

1. Wikipedia contributors. (2022, June 3). Fred Rogers. Wikipedia, The Free Encyclopedia. https://en.wikipedia.org/w/index.php?title=Fred*Rogers&oldid=1091237972*

Time Billionaire

1. Pompliano, A. (2020, December 7). Time billionaire. The Pomp Letter. https://pomp.substack.com/p/time-billionaire

Last Second Thoughts

1. [Analysis] Bus Accident Statistics in the United States. (2020, August 28). Paulsoncoletti.Com. https://www.paulsoncoletti.com/bus-accident-statistics/

Your Brain Is Your Ally, Not Your Enemy

1. Wikipedia contributors. (2022, June 2). Ten percent of the brain myth. Wikipedia, The Free Encyclopedia. https://en.wikipedia.org/w/index.php?title=Ten*percent*of*the*brain*myth&oldid=1091097929
2. Wikipedia contributors. (2022, March 29). MythBusters (2010 season). Wikipedia, The Free Encyclopedia. https://en.wikipedia.org/w/index.php?title=MythBusters(*2010*season)&oldid=1079942129
3. Boyd, R. (By Robynne Boyd on February 7 2008). Do people only use 10 percent of their brains? Scientific American. https://www.scientificamerican.com/article/do-people-only-use-10-percent-of-their-brains/
4. Storytellers. (2019, February 5). How to be Creative: Unleash Your Unconscious. Youtube. https://youtu.be/gVbd6aSNf38

For the Jacks

1. Cavendish, R. (n.d.). Daniel Defoe put in the pillory. Historytoday.Com. Retrieved June 14, 2022, from https://www.historytoday.com/archive/daniel-defoe-put-pillory

Don't 80/20 Your Dream

1. Wikipedia contributors. (2022a, April 19). Pareto principle. Wikipedia, The Free Encyclopedia. https://en.wikipedia.org/w/index.php?title=Pareto*principle&oldid=1083488474*

The Most Valuable Skill in the World

1. King, G. (2011, August 16). Charles Proteus Steinmetz, the wizard of Schenectady. Smithsonian Magazine. https://www.smithsonianmag.com/history/charles-proteus-steinmetz-the-wizard-of-schenectady-51912022/
2. Results for "What was a Dollar from the Past Worth Today?" (n.d.). Measuringworth.Com. Retrieved June 21, 2022, from https://www.measuringworth.com/dollarvaluetoday/relativevalue.php?year*source=1920&amount=10000&year*result=2022

Public Speaking for the Rest of Us

1. Feloni, R. (2017, September 16). Bridgewater founder Ray Dalio says he's going to take a lower profile once his book tours end. Business Insider. https://www.businessinsider.com/bridgewater-ray-dalio-going-dark-soon-2017-9
2. CNN. (2011, October 6). Steve Jobs' first TV interview. Youtube. https://www.youtube.com/watch?v=Eb9YTXmPolo

Perseverance

1. Neistat, C. (2016, August 9). 500K to 4 MILLION in 18 MONTHS. Youtube. https://www.youtube.com/watch?v=h0G3xFfhb94

Happiness Is Third Grade Math

1. What are the best one-minute life hacks? (n.d.). Quora. Retrieved June 27, 2022, from https://www.quora.com/What-are-the-best-one-minute-life-hacks/answer/James-Altucher

You Don't Need a New Thing to Be Grateful For

1. Altucher, J. (2015, July 6). Difficult gratitude. Medium. https://jaltucher.medium.com/difficult-gratitude-c3498250cda6

The Secret

1. Godin, S. (2017, November 6). This is post 7,000. Seth's Blog. https://seths.blog/2017/11/this-is-post-7000/

On Taking the Stairs

1. Ziglar, Z. (n.d.). A quote by Zig Ziglar. Goodreads.Com. Retrieved June 30, 2022, from https://www.goodreads.com/quotes/7557435-there-is-no-elevator-to-success-you-have-to-take
2. Neistat, C. (2015, April 8). Life Explained in 27 Seconds. Youtube. https://www.youtube.com/watch?v=L9VBpbnXhWk

The 30% Rule

1. Altucher, J. (2014, March 4). The ultimate cheat sheet for dealing with haters. James Altucher. https://jamesaltucher.com/blog/the-ultimate-cheat-sheet-for-dealing-with-haters/

The Isms That Ruin Your Judgement

1. Words that end in ism. (n.d.). Thefreedictionary.com. Retrieved July 19, 2022, from https://www.thefreedictionary.com/words-that-end-in-ism

You Can't Outrun Yourself

1. Ferriss, T. (2020, September 16). The Tim ferriss show transcripts: My healing journey after childhood abuse. The Blog of Author Tim Ferriss. https://tim.blog/2020/09/16/how-to-heal-trauma/

The Secret of a Happy Life

1. Wikipedia contributors. (2022, July 16). X-Men Origins: Wolverine. Wikipedia, The Free Encyclopedia. https://en.wikipedia.org/w/index.php?title=X-Men*Origins:*Wolverine&oldid=1098662138

Your Phone Should Be Like Your Toothbrush

1. How Much Time Does the Average Person Spend on Their Phone? (n.d.). KommandoTech. Retrieved July 26, 2022, from https://kommandotech.com/statistics/how-much-time-does-the-average-person-spend-on-their-phone/

When the Phone Rings

1. Behind the Brand. (2015, June 18). Seth Godin | How to make sure you NEVER get fired. Youtube. https://youtu.be/PJ6eZIYZsyg?t=39m1s

Be Water, My Friend

1. McBride, T. L. (2013, August 14). Bruce lee be as water my friend. Youtube. https://www.youtube.com/watch?v=cJMwBwFj5nQ

How To Not Waste Your Life

1. NetflixFilm. (2020, May 2). Tyler Rake is kicking ass. Twitter. https://twitter.com/NetflixFilm/status/1256407159471869954

Your Best Thought

1. Tseng, J., & Poppenk, J. (2020). Brain meta-state transitions demarcate thoughts across task contexts exposing the mental noise of trait neuroticism. Nature Communications, 11(1), 3480. https://doi.org/10.1038/s41467-020-17255-9
2. Google answers: Thoughts per day. (n.d.). Google.com. Retrieved August 3, 2022, from http://answers.google.com/answers/threadview/id/149262.html

Made in United States
Orlando, FL
26 September 2022